Warren Lamb
and Elizabeth Watson

Body code
The meaning in movement

Drawings by Clare Jarrett

Routledge & Kegan Paul
London, Boston and Henley

First published in 1979
by Routledge & Kegan Paul Ltd

39 Store Street,
London WC1E 7DD,

Broadway House,
Newtown Road,
Henley-on-Thames,
Oxon RG9 1EN and

9 Park Street,
Boston, Mass. 02108, USA

Set in 10/12 Linocomp Janson
and printed in Great Britain by
Lowe & Brydone Printers Ltd
Thetford, Norfolk

British Library Cataloguing in Publication Data
Lamb, Warren
    Body code.
    1. Nonverbal communication (Psychology)
    I. Title   II. Watson, Elizabeth
    301.14   BF637.C45   79-40489

ISBN 0 7100 0017 0

Contents

I

The secret language

Talk is modern man's remedy for every problem, his tool of communication in every situation. He 'gets around the table' with allies and enemies 'to negotiate', he 'chats up' his date, he 'shoots a line' to colleagues, 'gives his story' to the media and 'has it out' with his wife. He 'sells' a new line, 'makes his point', 'talks his way into – or out of – ' every conceivable situation and practises his word-power in a way that would make his silent rustic ancestors stare. Modern man, in fact, is a talkative animal, and if you ask him *how* he talks, he laughs instead. He knows we all talk, chatter, gossip, lecture and speak out most of the time – and yet for all that, *the majority of our 'talking' is done without speaking.*

Running along with our spoken words is a secret and mostly silent language which illustrates, fills out and annotates what we say. Some of it is not at all difficult to understand. We smile, nod, wink, wave, lift an eyebrow, frown, shake hands, drum our fingers and tap our feet

many times a week, using a silent shorthand of communication, which is easily interpreted: 'Hullo', we smile; 'OK', we nod; a wink, 'she did?'; a wave, 'he's off'; an eyebrow lifts, 'would you believe it?'; a frown, 'clear off'; a handshake, 'good to meet you'; tap-tap, 'I'm bored – or impatient'. We all make and translate dozens of such simple gestures each day, giving and reading them correctly within the context of our speech and actions. After all, there is nothing to a gesture. It delivers a message, but hardly one of deep meaning or significance, and although love and murder *have* followed a single gesture, we would be most surprised to obtain such results in anything but exceptional circumstances. Yet take a hundred – or a thousand – insignificant gestures together, and you find an invaluable, and infinitely variable, tool of communication.

For a start, the variety of possible gestures is immense. They are as varied as the hundreds-and-thousands used by bakers and confectioners, and generally we sprinkle them around without giving them much significance. 'Give our visitor a gesture of goodwill' usually produces a bunch of flowers, rather than a week in Paris. Even so, we cannot get along without them. They supplement our speech, bridge our silences, send unspoken messages, express our approval or contempt, or indicate our intention to speak next. Used this way, they cut

corners here and there and allow us to read the tone of the conversation or encounter as casual, cheeky, inviting, annoying, worrying or cheery, and they play a minor, although essential, role in our communication. But give them a break, and in no time they can take on much greater significance. When Churchill wanted to encourage a nation at war, he did not harangue the people at every appearance, he just gave the V-sign. This exceptional compression of a great deal of importance or feeling into a brief gesture is well understood, so much so that libellous tales of auctioneers, selling priceless works of art to penniless art-lovers nursing coughs, itches, colds or fidgets in the back row, are part of our folklore.

Outside the saleroom, however, gestures, even in numbers, generally express unimportant feelings and casual communications, for on most occasions a strong belief or feeling cannot easily be contained within a gesture or a series of specific gestures. It is only once in a while that we all agree to understand a great deal from a single gesture! People who express deep feeling or involvement may feel they are 'making a gesture', but in fact they are using their bodies quite differently and adopting an attitude or posture.

Anyone fretting over the latest international crisis knows that a diplomatic *gesture* can be safely ignored as a passing matter, whereas if his country adopts a *posture* on a disputed issue, this could be much more serious. This difference in meaning that we accept in the newspapers, applies also to the silent body language. Gesture is confined to a small part of the body, a shake of the shoulders, curl of the lips, furrowing of the brow, whereas adopting a posture requires every part of the body to be involved in tension. You can easily check this. Imagine you want to point out a parked car. All you need do is to raise your arm and hand into a pointing movement, while the rest of the body remains still. This is a gesture. But now imagine that the car is careering towards an unconscious friend. Immediately the pointing movement takes on urgency, and the tension involves the whole body, even if the movement throughout the head, trunk and limbs remains slight. You have adopted an attitude, or posture, of warning and the movement is no longer confined to a gesture.

So now we have been able to divide body language into two types which can be defined thus: gesture is movement confined to a part or parts of the body only; attitude or posture is movement involving the whole body.

This is a simple distinction. Try some experiments for yourself.

Suppose you are sightseeing with friends, and you want to show one of them something of particular interest. You beckon – a gesture which says 'Hi, John – or Mary – come and see this'. Then you realize that the subject of interest is fast disappearing over the horizon. You immediately adopt an attitude, or posture, which sends an urgent message, 'Hurry, hurry – here – quick!', taking up an attitude or posture of summons which involves your whole body, however slightly, whereas the first summons involved only a movement of arm or hand. You can think up dozens of situations like this where posture and gesture can be easily distinguished. Have you had a holiday abroad recently? Was your command of foreign languages shaky? Did you have an overfull car, too much luggage, an ambitious programme and an excellent appetite? Then you will recognize in the illustration

the signals commonly adopted by a tongue-tied expedition determined to secure the best in food, accommodation and travel facilities
from indifferent foreigners. You will easily be able to determine which
movements are postures and which gestures. You recognize only too
well the exaggerated postures that marked you as an eccentric mute,
and the bored gestures of your tolerant but bewildered hosts. Dividing
the movements into posture and gesture is easy. But these movements
in the illustrations have been selected and isolated just because they *do*
clearly illustrate the distinction between posture and gesture. A
family holiday conducted in sign-language is guaranteed to provide
exaggerated postures and gestures!

It is not always so easy. The difficulty begins when you set out to
observe the normal, unexaggerated movements of other people, and
try to analyse them. Suddenly there seems to be far too much movement all coming at once, shifting and blending continuously so that
you cannot say where that gesture – or was it posture? – began or
ended. Or, worse still, the movement is so restrained that you
cannot quite pinpoint it. If our premise that all bodily movement is
made up of posture and gesture is valid, then all these movements
must fall into one or other category. But it is so difficult to say which
with any degree of accuracy. What we need is an observation
technique – several if possible!

Fortunately this is not asking too much. Techniques for studying
body movement are already well developed. For example, those
movements that defied analysis, because they occurred too quickly,
give up their secrets quite readily if they are filmed. A slow play-back
of short excerpts of film untangles the mass of movements and permits
concentrated study. The observer can then make the distinction
between posture and gesture with certainty. There are also other
observation techniques which are particularly useful for recording
movements so slight that they are difficult to detect. Electromyography now allows us to feed signals from electrodes attached to
different parts of the body into a computer. The print-out then shows
clearly whether the parts of the body were acting together (posture), or
independently (gesture).

Techniques like these have immense implications for the study of
the silent language, and, as you would expect, non-verbal communication has recently attracted new emphasis and recognition. True, we
are all superficially aware of the body language of others and of the
messages sent out through our own body movements. But you don't

become an expert on fish by bobbing on the waves with boat and fishing line; you have to plunge right in with diving-suit and bathyscaphe! True, also, that some degree of understanding of the silent language goes back a long way. Certainly the ancient Greeks knew a good deal about body expression and its meaning. More recently, Charles Darwin applied the acute powers of observation that led him to develop his theory of evolution to the study of emotional expression. In 1872 he published *The Expression of Emotions in Man and Animals*, making use of fast-developing photographic techniques to record and analyse his evidence. After this, little of significance was published for nearly a century until in the late 1960s, non-verbal communication was suddenly 'discovered', and a spate of books appeared.

Much of this mass of research came to grief on a single but very rocky problem. A book called *Understanding Body Movement* by Martha Davis, published in 1972, with 900 bibliographic entries, demonstrates the ambitious scope of the research, and typical failure to grapple with this problem – a deceptively simple problem. For the problem was simply that much of the research did not deal with movement at all! Much of the description of movement was nothing of the sort; it described the *end results* of certain movements. For example, when a man puts his finger to his nose, it is not the final position of his finger which is the proper object of study, but the *process by which it got there* – the actual process of movement. Small wonder the researchers missed their target – because it is difficult to study movement and to collect data on it. How can behaviour, which is essentially movement, be recorded in a form which allows analysis, without destroying the quality of the movement? Or to take it more neatly and tunefully from *The Sound of Music*, 'How do you take a wave and pin it down?'

So back to the grass-roots, to the habitually perceptive people who consistently show a real facility for summing-up others, for forming accurate judgments of the motives, intentions, sincerity and such like of the people they meet. How do they explain their uncanny knack of 'reading' people correctly? Nine times out of ten they can't tell you. Usually they are at a loss for words, and the last thing in their minds is the problem of studying movement or pinning down waves. Still, if you press them, they may say, 'It was his manner that told me.' And there you have it. For, quite unconsciously, they have been exercising a gift for observing the way in which people use their bodies. They have spotted not so much *what* was done with the body, but *how* it was done. It is not the fixed position that has given them the vital clues but the movement leading to it. They are in fact, all unknowingly, connoisseurs of movement, experts in reading the secret language of the body – and you may very well be among them.

Whatever your present facility of perception, this book aims to enhance it by giving you the key to the secret language we call body language. With this key, you can begin to look at people in a new way, 'reading' them as easily by what they *don't* say as by what they tell you. The key lies in the distinction between posture and gesture, which focuses the attention on actual movement, rather than its completed result. By sharing with you discoveries based on the study of the postures and gestures of thousands of people in many parts of the world, this book offers you a new approach to understanding others. We cannot help but be involved in bodily expression, non-verbal communication, body language – call it what you like – every single day, unless we are hermits or recluses, and we have the essential key to the interpretation of this speaking silence in the distinction between posture and gesture. It is vital to our development of a gift for living that we learn to understand it!

2

The gist of gesture

Body language and the limitations of gesture

Hermits and recluses apart, we need to learn to understand body language. We have much to gain at work, at home, and at leisure, from learning to tune in on this secret unspoken communication. Let us begin with those actions that are confined to a part or parts of the body, which we have already defined as gestures. These make fascinating study in themselves, but we must always remember that, considered in isolation, they have a very limited contribution to make to non-verbal communication. Indeed, we have already agreed that a gesture is rarely performed in isolation, and only occasionally transmits any depth of feeling or information, since, as soon as there is any complicated meaning, the gesture can only be 'read' in relation to the whole expressive movement of the body. It must 'read' in relation to bodily posture. For example, for a cheery wave to *be* cheery, it must go along with an uplifted posture. If what we might have taken for a cheery wave is accompanied by a slumped posture, we are immediately confused, and read it for a pretence. We know it is not 'for real' because it looks incongruous, pathetic or comic. Whatever the effect may be on us, it is not likely to cheer us up, because the gesture is belied by the whole-man-in-action, just as it would be if someone, white with temper and gritting his teeth, were to give us a gentle shove or a tap on the shoulder. The gesture might be gentle enough, but a quick glance would soon convince us that for two pins our irate neighbour would gladly see us over the cliff edge, under a bus, or hammered into the ground. Far from hanging around in friendly *tête-à-tête*, we would be well advised to disappear smartly, unless we were prepared to slug it out on the spot.

A deliberate failure to match posture and gesture is part of the stock-in-trade of any comedian or clown. He shivers violently in an icy jet of water and keeps smiling, or merely lifts an eyebrow as a mouse runs up his trouser-leg. Comic zoo stories on the other hand rely on mistaken readings of animal gestures. The absurdity is in the unintentional failure to match posture and gesture. Any zoo-keeper could have told young Albert that he would end up as the lion's titbit if he persisted in thinking that the 'smiling' beast, tensing his muscles and swinging his tail in response to tickling with an umbrella, was

aiming to be his best friend. Similar stories of cuddly-looking pets with appetites for children are a commonplace nursery story joke. Those of us who would prefer to avoid such mistakes will play safe and remember, as we consider gestures in themselves, that in isolation from the whole-man-in-action – from posture – they may become quite meaningless.

Gesture interpretation and misreading

Unfortunately, all too many superficial studies of body language have done nothing of the kind, copying Albert's mistake with gusto. Like Albert, they fail to take the context of gesture into account, and like him they go down the wrong way. Here is a good example of gesture-misreading. Say I put my finger to the side of my nose? – immediately body language experts will 'read' my gesture as expressing doubt. But does it? Can you be sure? – of course not! Maybe my nose felt itchy, maybe I'm bored, maybe a thousand things – or nothing at all. There are after all another thousand ways in which I might have made this simple gesture. Did I do it quickly, slowly, strongly, lightly, twistedly, angular-fashion, via a forward-curved pathway or a sideways one, or what have you? *How* it was done, and what the rest of the body was up to at the time, tells far more, and gives innumerable possible variations of meaning, which cannot be conveyed by the gesture in isolation. Even suppose that we can show that a statistically significant number of finger-to-nose-putters *are* expressing doubt, where does that get us? There are bound to be so many exceptions to the rule, that this discovery would be useless, and since there are so many other ways of expressing doubt, not to mention the possibility that a doubter may not make a gesture at all, we can hardly link doubt to the finger-beside-the-nose. Finger-beside-nose = doubt is in fact a meaningless equation. If you want to know if someone is doubtful it would be far better to ask him. His reply is likely to be much more reliable than a superficial interpretation of one tiny gesture.

Trying to attribute a meaning to isolated gesture is like trying to survive Niagara in a barrel. (Why bother? – it's much more fun to watch.) Take smiling. Suppose your life-and-soul-of-the-breakfast-table companion catches sight of your hung-over, sleepy-eyed dourness between the folds of your paper, thumps the table vigorously and shouts to you to 'Cheer up under there – and for pity's sake smile'.

Incapable of manslaughter, or even a pat rejoinder, at such an hour, you may settle for a face-creasing contraction of the muscles by way of a smile, which, if you continue to feel morose, will scarcely be taken as a sign of your renewed enthusiasm. Of course, your bouncy friend *may* have an infectious influence, so that your gloomy expression changes for the better, but such a change involves an alteration of mood, not a mere stretching of mouth-muscles into the travesty of a smile. It may be a smiling gesture, but anyone can tell its not 'for real'. It does not convey any feeling that we would recognize as appropriate to this gesture.

Because most of us are quite good at detecting this degree of discrepancy between a gesture and its expected meaning, and can recognize the smile that *is* 'for real', those who think their jobs require a battery of smiles, or grew up to believe that 'the whole world loves a smile', might come on better without their grins. Like the 'smile' on Albert's lion, these meaningless gestures are incongruous, and incongruous behaviour can unnerve, terrify or give a cannibalistic impression. Outside the zoo, there are not many people with Albert's faith in smiles. Not all of us are ready to believe the smiling gentleman who says, 'I won't eat you.' Maybe he will! All the same, it is worth noting in passing, that the cult of the smile, perhaps above all in the USA, is a real red herring in the path of the would-be interpreter of body language. It is habitually, and often very skilfully, used to disguise what is really being 'said' in body language. And although we may not be taken in by a lion or a cannibal, we may very well be misled on other, less dramatic, occasions. The give-away, of course, is the contradiction between the smiling 'front', and a total posture indicative of feelings or mood that would not be expected to give rise to a smiling gesture. The gesture is clearly a lie, because the much more significant posture accompanying it is expressing something different. Anyone who perceives this contradiction will probably be very much disconcerted, although he will not be taken in. It would not do, obviously, to spend all day looking for the contradictions behind every smile. Most of them have to be taken on trust, and we would expect to respond to the superficial gesture. Nine times out of ten, it will not matter anyway, *but*, when we do want to make a deeper search for meaning, we should remember that the superficial gesture we call the smile is liable to take us in very easily. It's meant to!

Perhaps we are being rather hard on smiles. After all, many of our smiling gestures really do express some feeling that might appropriately be communicated by a smile, but this does not mean that we can immediately identify this feeling, and say just what it is. The Mona Lisa's smile is famous for its inscrutability. No one has ever been able to 'read' her gesture for certain, and this has given it an endless fascination. We cannot tell from the smiling gesture alone, whether it is radiating pleasure, or welcome, or acceptance, or superiority, or for that matter, any of the thousand and one meanings that might be expressed by a smile. It all depends, doesn't it? It depends *how* it is smiled and in what context, how it is culturally conditioned, and then again what code of interpretation the onlooker is using, since this may be both culturally orientated and individually biased. We may set out boldly to say smile-gesture =   but we land in a hole right away, as you can see from the gap in the print! This is not to say that miles of smiles come amiss. Deceptive or difficult to interpret they may be, but most of us prefer them to scowls. You might think we could easily agree with that statement, wouldn't you? After all, Edward Heath's sabre-toothed welcome, and Jimmy Carter's air of an engaging Father Christmas, were probably indispensable to their promotion to the national pedestal, and women with buck-teeth are said to want for neither popularity, employment nor husbands. But I am afraid it only goes to show how the simplest statement needs qualification, when it comes to examining gestures! Some years ago, it was generally said that the reigning Miss America would certainly have become Miss World if she had been able, just once in a while, to turn off her dazzling white smile. Too much sunshine and we have to get out our sunglasses – unless we are already on our envious way to the drugstore for toothpaste. Try as we may, there is only one thing we can say about a smiling gesture without being misleading, superficial, or inaccurate,

and that is that *no one can say for sure what it means.* You just can't read very much from the gesture *by itself.*

This may not seem a very earth-shaking conclusion, but in fact it is very significant. We have not wasted our time getting a close-up of the smile, because it is now apparent that if we are to progress with our grasp of body language and train ourselves to become more perceptive, we must examine gestures within their context. We have to recognize that gestures relate in certain ways to postures, tuning in with the environment to create the entire sequence of rhythmic movement, which is the whole-man-in-action. Within this flow of movement it is true that a small gesture, such as a nod, a wink, a raised eyebrow, might be highly significant, but it is significant as a part of the whole, and can only be interpreted in context.

Functional gesture

We have been forced to conclude that we cannot come up with reliable information based merely on a finger-by-the nose, a smile, or other limited action which makes an isolated gesture – unless, that is, we have overlooked a particular group of gestures to which this rule does not apply. We ought to consider whether *any* gesture, on its own, can *ever* give us reliable information. The pictures below provide the clue. Look at them and ask yourself what the gestures tell you. If you cannot

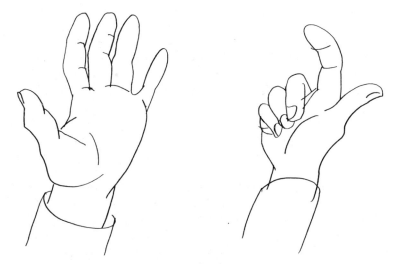

give an immediate and definite answer, you should never drive a car, or direct traffic. That is because you are looking at a *functional gesture*, and functional gestures should convey a precise message. Make a functional gesture yourself. Say, 'Over there, please; not there', and point to make your meaning clear. You will see at once that your pointing gesture can communicate such precise meaning, that your words can be left out altogether. A policeman on traffic duty must be an expert at this sort of gesture, and he relies on you, as driver, to interpret the meaning accurately. He is confident that you will be able to interpret a functional gesture correctly. You might even say he stakes his life on it. If you fail, the blow to him may be mortal, and the consequences to yourself are certain to spell disaster.

This disaster is very unlikely to happen to you. Like everyone else, you have learnt, somewhere on the way to your driving test, that a policeman's hand, presented in a semi-raised position with the palm flat towards you, means '*stop*'. A baby does not know this, and a five-year-old may not take any notice of it (ask any policeman), but, as adults, we take it for granted. It is a useful convention which we all find it convenient to accept. Even so, the accepted '*stop*' signal is carried out with varying degrees of precision. A driver holding up traffic because a tree has fallen across the road, or a workman holding it up while shouting to his mates, may not signal as clearly as an experienced policeman, and even an experienced policeman's gestures will vary if he is cross or tired. Most of us can spot this at once. His signals may vary too, according to the suppleness of limb, or the pace at which the oncoming traffic is threatening him. But when all this variation is allowed for, there still is a well-recognized gesture which means '*stop*'. And whereas we *cannot* say: finger-to-nose=expression of doubt, we *can* say: presentation of palm in semi-raised position= signal to stop.

Gesture and convention

You may now be feeling the relief of the pedestrian who makes it to a traffic island in the rush hour, or finds himself standing on the *welcome* mat at the pub after a long walk uphill. 'A certainty at last', you may be thinking, 'I've got the gist of gesture'. Well, like the chap on the traffic island, we *are* halfway across, but it's too soon to relax. We have to plunge back into the traffic to reach the other side and that *welcome* mat is slipping a bit. We have to bear in mind that a common understanding of gesture presupposes a similar cultural understanding. Even within a culture, accepted gestures may easily be misunderstood. For instance, Italians wave goodbye with a gesture that would bring neighbouring Europeans running to see what was wanted. They would read this gesture as a beckoning one. The case is much more obvious when we consider cultures quite different to our own. There are certainly cultures into which we could drop our policeman where all his experience could not prevent him puzzling the natives with his efficient 'stop' signals. On this occasion, he would be much more likely to be bowled over than if you and I were approaching a crossroads from opposite directions!

There is a legendary account of the voyages of Captain Cook which illustrates cultural conditioning. It is said that when Captain Cook landed on the Fiji islands' beach and walked to meet an oncoming band of natives, he thrust out his hand in token of friendship. It never occurred to him that an offer to shake hands could be interpreted as a threatening gesture, because his countrymen were all conditioned to 'read' his gesture as friendly. In the split second of his action, however, the natives, who were *not* so conditioned, interpreted the thrust of hand and arm as an aggressive action, and promptly killed the explorer. Legend has it that before he made his gesture they were ready to be friendly; they just did not know about the conventional gesture we call a handshake.

Now, most of us are not going to come to a sticky end because someone misinterprets our gestures. All the same, miscommunication by gesture is very common even within our culture, and leads to all sorts of irritation, annoyance, and misunderstanding. Proper reading of gestures depends, as we have discovered, on understanding the underlying convention. This would all be plain sailing if only you could be sure of your convention. But the trouble is that convention is not really static, even when it appears to be. Like our *welcome* mat it is inclined to be on the move; just as you think you can rely on it, it slips and catches you unawares. This is because, even within a particular society, convention is constantly evolving. So that, although we find it very convenient to agree that certain gestures have certain well-understood functions, we cannot quite take this for granted. Inevitably we misread each other's signals. Somehow, the form of gesture, or the way we made it, has conveyed to others something we didn't quite intend.

This is particularly evident across the more obvious divisions in society, such as the generation gap. The young adapt conventional gestures to their own use, modifying them, and using them with a subtle new emphasis, which their elders may read as insolent, indifferent, or undisciplined. They in turn are misread. Their careful, crabbed, or fussy gestures, not greatly, but vitally, different from those of their grandchildren, mark them out as reactionary, dictatorial, or rigid to the oncoming adventurers. Even that most conventional of friendly gestures, the handshake, may not be interpreted as a friendly gesture by the recipient. Again it depends how, and in what context, the shaking is done. Perhaps it was not only the natives who found Captain Cook's handshake aggressive? Many a hostess, nursing fingers into which her rings have been savagely driven, has wondered whether her male friends were communicating friendship or machismo. This is why we cannot rely altogether on convention, even within our own culture. We cannot say: gesture of handshake = act of friendship. There are altogether too many variables!

Gesture variation – voluntary and involuntary

We are, in fact, only just beginning to scratch the surface of possible gesture variation, because up till now, we have assumed that gestures are *voluntary*, whereas clearly this is not always so. Any of the gestures

we have already examined may be performed with varying degrees of volition, and their character will alter accordingly. Your smile, as I come to meet you, may be a voluntary politeness, resulting from your good breeding, excellent upbringing, and careful training, but it will change to the involuntary grin of the untutored savage if I slip on a banana skin as I bound forward. Alternatively, your involuntary smile, as you recognize a born banana-skin-rider, may change to a voluntary smile of grim satisfaction if you arranged the environment on purpose to suit my talents. In this case you are using the same smiling gesture both voluntarily and involuntarily.

Some gestures, however, start and continue *involuntarily*, and these include finger fidgets and facial mannerisms. You might suppose that an involuntary gesture would be easy to interpret, because we can catch it unawares, in the raw. It cannot be concealed or disguised. For instance, we may confidently label fidgets and twitches as 'nervous' mannerisms, but we are unlikely to get away with it. Friends who drum the table or doodle on their pads will flatly deny nervousness, and demand with justifiable heat our reasons for making such a deduction from their fidgets. But perhaps we can be more confident in interpreting involuntary expressions of liking and dislike? You might hope to look round a cafe and say which customer was enjoying the food by glancing at his facial expression. Unfortunately, if you don't know the customers personally, you are probably wrong. Aunt Agatha wore a disgusted expression while enjoying her last birthday treat, and our saintly vicar looks benign over his tripe. As with

functional gestures, there is a lot of scope for misinterpretation, particularly as expressive gestures are closely allied to those which arise
involuntarily in response to bodily sensations, such as an itch, an ache,
or maybe just wind. We will probably be both inaccurate and annoying in taxing the fidgety fellow with poor nerves – whatever that may
mean – and we risk looking ridiculous if we join behaviourists in a
search for some deep significance behind a gesture that probably only
indicates too much acid in the stomach.

Habit-based, or culturally-conditioned gesture

On the other hand, the study of another type of gesture, which we
might describe as the habit-based gesture, yields a great deal of
valuable data to the serious researcher. We have already seen how
important cultural conditioning can be in deciding our reaction to
gestures such as the policeman's '*stop*' signal, or a friend's handshake;
now we need to look more closely at the nature of these culturally
conditioned, or habit-based gestures, if only to prevent us making all
sorts of unwarranted and absurd assumptions, as soon as we take a step
away from the familiar territory of our own culture. In an ever-shrink-
ing world, in which cultures increasingly overlap, more and more of us
are called upon, in business, on holiday, in diplomacy, in politics and
at social functions, to avoid, to put it at its least, the sort of mistakes
in gesture-reading which may result in unfortunate incidents. These
may be merely amusing, but may well prove as damaging to business
or diplomacy, or even as fatal to our purposes as the failure of the
natives to read Captain Cook's handshake as a gesture of friendship.

Even in Europe, where many of us like to feel 'at home' on occasion,
we are liable to come running when an Italian is waving goodbye,
because the gesture seems to beckon, or mistake the vigorous gestures
that accompany banal talk for signs that the subject is arousing great
feeling or interest. How much more confusing things become when
we set out for India, or for Russia, or for the East, a difficulty often
compounded by the overlaying of the traditional gestures of the
indigenous culture by gestures borrowed from the West! When
gestures borne of long tradition are performed within a culture that is
rapidly changing, there is often a degree of hesitancy in their performance. It is as though the performer feels that his gestures are
inappropriate to new situations and conditions, but dares not risk

excluding them, just as the home-coming schoolboy dare not miss giving a tug at a certain bush or other such ritual gesture, for fear of the avenging fates and the immediate onset of a thousand misfortunes! In the same way the Japanese will often perform some semi-bow or head-nodding that derives from an ancient hierarchical culture in which humility was wise, and the lack of a humble appearance might be fatal. The semi-bow and the nod are retained today, although the need for humility has disappeared. None the less, the gesture is misleading to those of other cultures. The Western businessman is in danger of thinking that his Japanese counterpart *is* humble because he *looks* humble, even though a moment's reflection would convince him otherwise. He is deceived by the appearance of humility, while himself adopting the habit-based, 'correct' stance of the dynamic Western entrepreneur, hoping that the forward thrust of his chin and the vigorous handshake will convey dynamism and firmness, regardless of his real temperament or attitude. It remains, however an open

question which of the two is in fact the more aggressive and dynamic; the habit-based gestures are not an adequate guide. Moreover, such gestures can be adapted to mean whatever their performer wishes. It depends how he chooses to relate them to his other body movements. Imagine a 'humble' bow involving only the upper part of the body, with no movement of the legs, but with a slight smiling gesture of the mouth and a sidelong glance at a colleague! This is far more likely to express a mocking superiority than humility, and the more exaggerated because of the disharmony between the traditional meaning of the gesture and its actual performance.

It would be equally unwise to assume that Russians are more affectionate than other nationalities because they frequently greet each other with a kiss on both cheeks. What can we tell from this habit-based gesture? The answer is: nothing. The kissing is no more than a gesture, carrying so little meaning in itself that it might very well be *more significant when omitted* than when performed. Its *non-performance* might tell you something about a Russian's enemies, that its performance would not tell you about his friends. It is as difficult to read significance into the kiss-greeting in itself as to give interpretation to the Indian custom of placing the hands together in a gesture of prayer, and gently moving them up and down. The meaning of this gesture – or the lack of it – depends on the way in which it is performed. The 'humble' Japanese bow, the 'affectionate' Russian greeting, and the 'gentle' Indian welcome have all become so hallowed by tradition that they cannot be read as 'humble', 'affectionate' or 'gentle' with any assurance, and they can be converted to express something quite different if the performer so wishes, either by the manner of the performance or its context. In the immensely popular war film of experiences in the Far East, *The Bridge over the River Kwai*, there was a scene in which the Japanese prison-camp commander faced the inmates with the intention of disciplining them. The prisoners' leader broke ranks and kissed him, and by this one inappropriate gesture, deflected all the commander's anger from the men to himself, breaking his authority and making him lose face so badly that the authorities were forced to relieve him of his position. Nobody 'read' this gesture as affectionate, just as, at the other end of the scale, a full-blooded kiss on the lips, when a kiss on both cheeks had been expected, would hardly be dismissed as a sign of mere affection. Once again, the meaning is not in the gesture itself. *It all depends on how and when it is performed.*

To the expert, the study of culturally conditioned gestures is as revealing as the study of speech was to Professor Higgins in George Bernard Shaw's play *Pygmalion*. In his book *Kinesics and Context*, an important contribution in this field, Professor R. L. Birdwhistell shows that, just as the dialect-orientated Professor Higgins could demonstrate that people betray their class and provenance by their speech, so the expert in body language can demonstrate that people reveal the culture to which they belong – and of course their place in that culture – by the gestures they use. Gestures are convincingly shown by Professor Birdwhistell to be culturally conditioned. If it were possible for us all to become experts in recognizing gestures and their significance in different cultures, we would be able to astonish our friends by confidently asserting that this person sniffing at us over here is expressing disapproval, and is on the verge of laying about us, whereas this other sniffer is expressing contempt and is about to shake our dust off his heels. Neither sniffer, we can insist, are suburban sniffs of the sort analysed by the happy-ever-after-I-used-deodorant variety so prized by advertisers. But, experts or no, at the very least we shall be aware that our relationships with others will be very much affected by whether or not we belong to the same cultural group. Within such a group, gestures can be exchanged in the sure knowledge that they will be understood aright, because the group has a common gestural alphabet. Outside the cultural group, many of these gestures have to be abandoned, either because they would carry no meaning, or because they would be misread. Even if we cannot become experts in interpretation, an appreciation of the culture-based nature of gesture would prevent the worst mistakes and help us to avoid howling errors of tact or social solecisms.

To sum up – gesture needs a background

Hazards beset anyone who hopes to attribute meanings to gestures. Gestures form a convention, or culture-based alphabet, which we use one way in private, yet another way within our own cultural group, and yet again in other ways with people different to ourselves, especially in situations outside our usual experience. Attempts to publish a gesture-alphabet, to say gesture X = this, whereas gesture Y = that, will always prove misleading unless the definitions cover a whole range of variables. We can begin to make allowance for these variables as soon as we begin to perceive gestures in relation to their context. Such a context is provided by the background, as it were, of the body, on which the gestures happen. The smallest twitch of an eyebrow is, in fact, only significant *in relation to the body posture on which it takes place*. We need to study this relationship, but of course we are not yet in a position to do so. It takes more than one to make a relationship, and so far we have given a lot of consideration to gesture and none to posture. Posture deserves study in its own right.

3

The place of posture

'Making' a gesture and 'having' a posture

What then is the nature of the relation between posture and gesture? Perhaps we could describe it in terms of 'having' and 'making'. For instance, I have a good sense of direction, but no feel for numbers; you may have a flair for cooking, but no feel for machinery; or a talent for administration, but no gift for writing poetry; or a good ear for music, but no colour sense. Between us we make, as a result of this 'having', well-planned journeys, scrambled accounts, divine dinners, scrap-iron of the lawn mower, a smooth-running business, doggerel, beautiful tunes, and a disaster of the bathroom decorations. What we make depends on what we have; the making derives from the having. In just the same way, gesture is dependent on, and derives from, posture.

The same analogy also highlights the distinction between posture and gesture. We do not *make* a posture, in the way that we make a gesture of the hand, or face, or some other part of the body. A posture is not something that we make at all, for the simple reason that we already have it. We *have* a posture which is natural to us, and except in so far as we might modify it by our own efforts, we have to live with it. This natural posture of ours decides how we perceive the world about us. Take a very large-scale example, and this is immediately apparent! Consider how very differently the world must have appeared to the hominid that went on all fours and to the primeval man who, in the course of evolution, learned to stand upright. To the upright man, the world must have looked, felt, and been open to examination, exploration, and manipulation, in a way impossible to a creature carrying its head at a lower level, and lacking the full use of hands. In a lesser degree, but in much the same way, the world is perceived differently by individuals with different postures. The astrologer in *Aesop's Fables*, walking with the habitual posture of a star-gazer, did not see the well at his feet. Of the two proverbial beggars, the one with the braced-back shoulders and an upward gaze saw stars, where his fellow with the bowed head and rounded shoulders saw mud.

Posture adjustment

It is, however, a mistake to think of posture in one form only. To some extent we can all modify and adjust our posture, so that the astrologer may become more bowed, while the bowed beggar becomes less so. This is the same as with other things that we 'have'. An ear for music can be cultivated, a flair for cookery developed, and a sense of direction encouraged. The degree and speed of alteration depends on the individual's capacity for modification, or, to put it differently, his range of postural adjustment. If the individual is a youth, and his postural habit less deeply ingrained, he may alter quite quickly from the downcast, drooping victim of school bullies, to an upstanding outward-looking member of the armed forces, so that on his first few visits home, friends and relatives will say that the army has 'made a new man of him'. But the long-service beggar and the astrologer are

unlikely to bring about so dramatic a modification. In fact, such modifications of posture have definite limits. Just as our aptitude for cookery, or music, or orienteering, is not altered outright by cultivation, development, or encouragement, so an adult's natural posture, or posture profile, is susceptible to adjustment, but not to radical change.

This capacity to modify posture is illustrated by very many phrases in the English language which suggest attitudes achieved through postural adjustment, rather than fixed forms of posture. Here are some of them: standing one's ground, head in the clouds, head first, feet first, backing down, knocking someone off their feet, digging in one's heels, with open arms, at arm's length, rising to the occasion.

Clearly, achieving any one of these postures will be easier for some than for others. 'Standing one's ground', for example, may be much easier for you than for your friend, because this particular attitude is more characteristic of you as an individual, and can be more easily blended with your natural posture, or existing posture profile. This adjustment comes more 'naturally' to you than to him. But your friend may look more natural with a 'head in the clouds' attitude than you do, because it is more characteristic of *him*, and more closely in line with *his* posture profile. This modification is more within his capacity – and less within yours – because of the different postures you have to start with. Individual posture profiles have varying capacity for modification – their own adjustment range – but do not change outright, any more than a dog walking on its hind legs ceases to be a dog. Nothing is easier than an outright change of gesture – a victory gesture can be changed into an insult simply by reversing the hand – but once postural habits become entrenched, there is no evidence that significant change, as opposed to adjustment, is possible under normal circumstances. A dog may walk on his hind legs, but he cannot lose his 'dogginess'; you do not catch him balancing on his forepaws. Like our shadow, our posture profile keeps us company whether we like it or not. It is part of us.

Posture interpretation and prejudice

Not only does our posture profile stick by us, it continually 'talks' of us through the secret language of our movement, so that it can be understood by others. Each posture profile is unique to the individual, and expresses itself in a meaningful way, and it would be easier for us to interpret this postural expression if the ground were not already littered with inadequate attempts to do so. We have to examine some of these before our way is clear.

Because the condition of the skeleton and the muscles attached to it obviously influences movement, there have been many attempts to 'read' people by their physique. For example, you notice that someone is tall and thin, and so you 'read' him as a brainy, nervous, introverted person. There are excellent precedents around for this type of psycho-physical judgment. The ancient Hindu method of classifying people by castes, the medical classifications of the Greek doctor Hippocrates, and more recently the classifications devised by Kretschmer, Stockard, Viola and Dr William Sheldon, have all been based on the belief that certain temperamental tendencies match certain types of physique – or somato types, as they are called. New versions of this theory have been continually expounded and developed since the heyday of the Greeks and before, but unfortunately their antiquity would seem to be greater than their accuracy, and they are not borne out by the findings of modern investigations and research.

It has been shown that people of similar skeletal and muscular build do not move in similar ways, so that there are as many exceptions to the equation; tall and thin = brainy, nervous and introverted, as there are people who conform to it. The exception may prove the rule, but too many exceptions prove the rule worthless. It would seem that, on the evidence now available, any simple matching of somato types with temperamental characteristics has to be abandoned. Postural expression cannot be 'read' from type of physique – it is an even bet that we are quite wrong if we assume that all small, fat men are jolly and officious, or that all tall men are withdrawn and crafty. *These are psycho-physical prejudices.*

These prejudices are deeply rooted in our culture, and the more so because they have been around a long time. How easy do you find it to visualize Father Christmas as tall, thin, and with high-domed forehead, or Christ as short and fat? We expect the slim, delicately boned child to be chosen to play the Virgin Mary in the school Nativity play, and to find the dowager duchess of sixth-form comedy massively built, red of face, and powerful of eye. More, we would assume that the first *was* kind and good, and the second bossy and overbearing, because they 'look it', just as a 'good' soldier is muscular and broad-shouldered, the 'dutiful' arm of the law is issued with big feet, and the 'kind' nanny is plump and broad of beam.

We are confirmed in these prejudices by sharing them with the best people! Shakespeare has Julius Caesar say:

Let me have men about me that are fat
Sleek-headed men, and such as sleep o'night.
Yon Cassius has a lean and hungry look,
He thinks too much: such men are dangerous.

The combined authority of the Shakespeares and Caesars strengthens our prejudices, and explains why, in everyday life, we are so often surprised when we 'get to know' people: 'He's not like that at all'; 'She's all right when you get to know her'; 'You'd never think it to look at him!'; 'She's quite different really'. These startled comments come from our personal experience, and experience is a poor liar.

If our experience is wide enough to take us outside our own culture, we more easily recognize our assumptions for *cultural prejudices*, because we find that they are not universally shared. It helps to remember that the Buddha is depicted as mountainously fat; that Tongan men and women receive approval in direct proportion to their weight; and that a trustworthy Italian has 'good bottom', showing him to be no fly-by-night but a man of weight and importance. (For the Italian the test of worth is his inability, when standing with his heels against a wall, to touch his toes without falling on his face. If his action forces him away from the wall, he is a man of substance in every sense.) It is apparent from these examples that different societies, tribes, and cultures 'read' posture profiles to suit their own psycho-physical prejudices, giving different physical traits desirability or acceptability ratings that we would not accord, and matching temperament and type of physique in ways alien to our own culture. Clearly, if we hope to get a true reading from posture, we must see these prejudices for what they are, and abandon the attempt to obtain it from the evidence of physique.

It is difficult to purge our reading of posture from cultural prejudice, because we are usually unaware that we are making assumptions. When a Western official went to a Chinese village to talk to the women about birth control, he was surprised by the bewildered silence that followed his lecture. Finally a woman rose to her feet and after thanking him courteously regretted that due to a misunderstanding his time had been wasted. Did he not know that most of his audience were married? A similar silence greeted the Westerner who recounted the story of Shakespeare's *Hamlet* to an African tribe, among whom it was customary, and indeed a pious duty, to marry the widow of a deceased brother! It is all too easy to make assumptions, and these are plentiful not only between cultures but nearer home.

Just as it is difficult to purge our reading of posture from culturally induced prejudice, so it is difficult to rid it of those which are more personal to ourselves. When we look at someone and describe him as 'having his head in the clouds', there is a large element of *personal interpretation* in this judgment with which others may not agree. To them, this posture may seem buoyant. This is highlighted if we try to interpret not only our neighbour's head-in-the-clouds posture, but those of persons divided from us by many generations or large tracts of time. It then becomes apparent that our prejudices about posture arise not only from the person we happen to be, but also from the times in

27

which we live. The posture that the Greeks felt to be the height of manfulness would be regarded by many today as effeminate, while the martial bearing of the Romans would probably appear pompous. A Christ-like posture can embody a wide range of meanings from compassion and gentleness to power and asceticism, depending to some extent on the onlooker's point of view. The usually depicted posture of Napoleon now looks ridiculous in its fixed form, but neither he, nor his portrait, seem to have appeared absurd to his contemporaries, not even, so far as we know, to his enemies. It is because we live in other times that we perceive it otherwise. We cannot escape *generation-prejudice*.

Interpretative tools

Of course, we are badly handicapped in judging postures from past eras, because the evidence is limited to sculpture, portrait, and whatever we are able to reconstruct from written descriptions. Matters have been much better since the advent of film; we have evidence of the way in which people move their bodies in assuming postures. We can watch them take up an attitude, hold it, break it, and renew it in a new form, and we get some clue as to their emotions. We can tell, as they are filmed taking up these attitudes, whether they were anxious, joyful, despairing, uplifted or angry or what you will. No doubt Napoleon was capable of all these emotions, but his stereotyped portrait gives us no clue at all. We can see the fixed posture but without any variation, and so we cannot perceive his posture profile.

Welcome though the film is as an aid to interpreting posture, it brings us up against a new difficulty if it has a soundtrack. For our purposes the spoken word is a red herring. We must not allow ourselves to be influenced by words which may be quite at variance with what is being 'said' in the silent language. You come across this contradiction often enough in everyday life. Someone steps on your foot in passing and apologizes. He says, 'I'm sorry', but with an angry or arrogant posture. Do you suppose for one moment that he is really sorry? Of course not! You perceive the contradiction between the words and the posture at once, and you automatically discount what has been said. You take it that the true meaning is in the silent language of posture. However, in less clear-cut cases, it may be less easy to discount the spoken word, because the situation involves more people, and because what is expressed, both verbally and non-verbally, is more complicated. Here again, films are an immense aid to investigation, because they can be run without the soundtrack. Let us throw on the screen a soundless film of a politician haranguing a stormy meeting. We do not know what he is saying, but we can see that every line of him proclaims anxiety. He is Mr Doom-and-gloom in person! To be sure he must be proclaiming the loss of a major war, the ruin of the economy, or some other armageddon! No wonder his hearers are so excited! We now restore the soundtrack and give the film a re-run.

To our amazement, we hear our orator proclaiming with all possible confidence and emphasis that we've never had it so good. Utopia has arrived! It's all found from now on – and the crowd are impatient to find it. But, if we have any sense, we will ask ourselves why our politician is so anxious, and stay behind to ask some questions. His posture gives the lie to his assertions.

Conventional requirement and postural habit

Film is also an invaluable aid when we try to examine the effect on posture of *conventional requirements*. The worthy Greek citizen, the Roman soldier, and the powerful emperor, are presented to us in fixed postures; we can see that postural norms must have changed, since their day, but cannot study the full range and significance of this discovery. Our grandfathers and grandmothers cannot escape us in this way! There they are on film, under our scrutiny, and it is clear at once that conventional posture requirements have changed dramatically ever since the beginning of this century. We see that half a century or so ago an exaggerated postural dignity was demanded in all public appearances, because people were expected to carry themselves in public in a manner that demonstrated a particularly important role or position in society. Not only were strict, conventional requirements in dress enforced, but no relaxation was permitted from the dignified attitude prescribed by convention as normal public posture. For this reason films, and to a lesser extent photographs, can be easily dated. Those unsmiling – even daunting – photos of somebody's Uncle George, the industrial magnate; or Uncle Henry, the political leader; or Sir Edward Bloggs, surgeon of First World War fame; which show the men in ramrod stance, with fierce glare and belly thrust aggressively forward, can only belong to an era which demanded of its leading men that they should look authoritative and well-to-do. Films of their peers and colleagues allow us to study the full range of socially acceptable posture in this period.

Today, in a more equal society, the requirement is different. Photos show leaders in attitudes that the onlooker feels might easily be his own. Mr Wilson sucks his pipe, Mr Heath helms a boat, Mrs Thatcher waves cheerily, and the Queen walks her dogs and decorates a Christmas tree. Films confirm and fill out the evidence for this new concept of desirable posture. It is not the individual posture that is significant, but that the fact that the mass of attitudes conform to this requirement. People whose grandfathers were scorners of easy chairs and smiles, the terror of babies, and never to be seen in any domestic action, let alone any vice like smoking, now have the posture profile of the loller in deck-chairs, the smiling man of mackintosh and pipe, the indefatigable baby-kisser, the lover of dogs and do-it-yourself. For our grandfathers, a posture profile that we would regard as pompous was mandatory, while our own postural norms of compliance, relaxation and hail-fellow-well-metness would have scandalized our worthy ancestors.

Posture has changed to meet a changed convention, but we must not be deceived by its new easy-going appearance. The new postural convention is just as binding on us, in our own times, as it was on our forebears, and binding not only in the sense of being required, but also

in the sense that once it is built in to our natural posture, it is susceptible to adjustment but not to change. It becomes part of us. This is perhaps even more dramatically illustrated in women than in men. That ramrod photo of great-grandmother, stern of eye, mouth like a vice, legs tensed together, hands folded, reflects not merely her authority over her household, but a severe ideal of motherhood, coupled with a denial of sexuality. The attitudes of her grand-daughter, however, demonstrate in photo and film, with wide gestures of the limbs, a smiling face, and a relaxed stance, a combination of a sense of equality with the repudiation of authority, and a sense of the need to be popular, while not suffering under any rigid sexual taboo. Now imagine for a moment that, by some ghastly trick of a time-machine, the girl finds herself in her great-grandmother's place and the great-grandmother is suddenly propelled into our own times. Both will try to adjust their postures to the conventional requirements so horribly thrust on them by fate, and probably the great-granddaughter will be the more successful of the two, but it is unlikely that their new worlds will ever approve of them as 'genteel lady' or 'a real good kid', because their posture profiles can be adjusted, but not changed. Indeed, individuals have varying degrees of success in meeting the posture requirements of their own generation.

31

Postural adjustment range and the capacity to conform

Depending on their individual characteristics, some individuals can absorb the conventional norm of their generation into their posture-profile more easily than others, since the profile is predisposed towards dignity and severity, or to relaxation and approachableness, as the case may be. Within the limits of individual capacity the degree of effort to conform to the social convention will vary according to the severity of the penalties for non-conformity and the rewards consequent on obtaining social approval. Such rewards and penalties are no trifling matters, and involve not only the general approval that surrounds the individual during upbringing and education and in casual everyday contacts, but also acceptance or rejection in employment, marriage, and social prestige. Money, sex and position are contingent on social approval, while among the penalties for deviation are loneliness, humiliation, loss of opportunities for wealth and sex satisfaction, and the position of social outcast or pariah. The emphasis will be different in different generations and the severity less in tolerant times, but the pressure to conformity is always present. In this conformity test, it is particularly true that 'every dog has his day'. In war-torn times the man who looks 'every inch' a soldier, in times of feminine dependency the appearance of the sweet idiot, in times of social inequality the grandly authoritarian, and in democratic times the popularly co-operative, have the individual posture characteristics that bring approval.

Let us conceive these characteristics as a line stretching from maximum unpopularity at one extreme to maximum acceptability at the other:

less socially acceptable − ——————— + more socially acceptable.

If this line is divided into 10 units between these extremes, we can show the individual ratings accorded by society to the individual characteristics of a selection of its members.

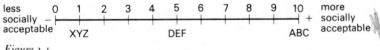

Figure 3.1

In Figure 3.1 A, B and C are born lucky. In their generation, they have posture profiles which coincide naturally with society's requirements, as a twig might grow naturally where the gardener wished it to be.

These fit the 'ideal' man or woman of their time. No pressure to conformity is felt by them, no effort towards conformity exerted, and they receive maximum approval for as long as the conventional posture requirement remains the same. When it changes, they will probably continue to have the approval of their contemporaries, but not of the younger generation. DEF are less lucky. They are poised between extremes, receiving approval and pressure to conform about equally. They must adjust, but not too severely. Reasonable effort will bring them within reach of the ideal, as a twig might be gently coaxed into place. XYZ, however, are born with individual posture characteristics which bring maximum social disapproval, and must adjust to survive, or be forced into a deviant out-group. This would apply to effeminate men, and masculine women, in most generations, but other characteristics would depend on the current ideal. In another society or time, the characteristics of XYZ might be the very ones to win maximum approval. For example, in times of maximum female dependency, the full score might be accorded to the empty-headed scatterbrained posture, but in a pioneering community this might score 0, and an aggressive posture, scoring 0 in the conservative society, might score 10 in the pioneering situation. Such persons often win the approval of the new generation, who bring in a new convention more suited to their natural posture profiles. Meanwhile, the pressure on them is severe, as on a twig which must come into line or be cut away.

The individual capacity to adjust limits the individual adjustment range but the use made of it depends on the degree of willingness, and the amount of social pressure applied. The arrows on Figures 3.2 and 3.3 measure the effort to adjust, according to capacity.

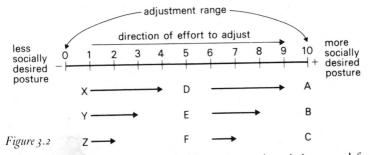

Figure 3.2

In Figure 3.2 D and X are probably women, since it is normal for society to demand greater conformity to the 'ideal woman' than to the 'ideal man'. Both, having similar capacity and applying similar effort, succeed in adjusting by 5 points, but this adjustment which brings D to the ideal, leaves X half-way. E and Y apply less effort, or have less capacity to adjust, which leaves E not too far from the ideal but Y too far away for comfort, although both have shifted by 3 points. F moves only one point, but still remains 5 points ahead of Z who will not, or cannot, adjust significantly, and remains outside the social pale.

Feminine posture and clothes

Whatever the other variables affecting the amount of pressure towards conformity, the greatest effort (the longest arrows) will apply to the women, from whom a greater degree of conformity is exacted, and for whom operating at the less socially desirable end of the scale is less tolerated and more heavily penalized. She must move farther from being 'herself', and nearer to being the 'ideal woman', and the degree of strain depends on how nearly in tune with the convention her natural posture is at the start. Sometimes, indeed, mere conformity of posture is not enough. She must go beyond her capacity for posture adjustment – from conformity to deformity – in the struggle to meet social requirements.

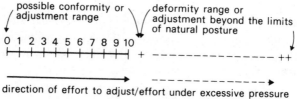

Figure 3.3

Genuine anatomical deformity has been brought about in our own culture by mechanical means such as tight lacing, corsets, high heels and pointed shoes. These have actually altered the bone structure. In other cultures the more extreme examples are of course the giraffe-necked beauties of Burma or the bandaged lily-feet of the Chinese aristocrat – mechanical aids have also been used, rather less fanatically, to bring about conformist rather than deformed posture, such as backboards, weights suspended from the neck, and exercise routines.

Clothes have been used to bring about both the 'appearance' of deformity, as witness the bustle, or to emphasize conformity to the ideal, which may at times be the ideal of self-sufficiency or emancipation. If fertility is valued, as in the thirteenth century and early Tudor times, then women stand with bellies prominent, and dresses are gathered to a high bodice to give emphasis to the possibility of pregnancy, or, if motherhood rather than fertility is the ideal, and sex

is 'out', then the crinoline both keeps the men at bay, and emphasizes the hips – the strangulation of the waist also serving this purpose. If sex is permissive, and emancipation is looked for, then the body is merely draped, and those draperies may outline or reveal the natural woman, as after the French Revolution, or as today, when women wear draped, natural styles out of working hours, but at work are dressed for economic self-sufficiency. At other times the bandaged bust and boyish look puts motherhood at a distance, while perilous silk stockings or hobble skirts reflect a compliance with economic dependency, since neither leg fashion allows for competitive work, but is designed to handicap activity. Similarly high heels throw woman as a sex-symbol into prominence, as witness the bunny girl, chorus girl or usherette, whose dress is of particular interest since the appearance of sexual and economic dependence is actually enlisted as an aid to its opposite – an independent wage. Clothes are in fact invaluable in aiding and abetting woman's struggle to achieve the socially desired posture, particularly where the lack of it must be heavily concealed.

Posture adjustment and individual characteristics

The greater the requirement to adjust to the conventional posture norm, the more apparent refusal to do so becomes. Although women have now adopted Bloomer dress, modernized, as *de rigueur*, Amelia Bloomer and her followers scored o on the Victorian scale. Such rebels realized that to adopt the habitual posture of compliance, or foolish helplessness, or submissiveness, actually developed these qualities. The adjustment of posture in these directions influences self-expression and works on the self, emphasizing those individual characteristics that accord most easily with the movement to conformity. A society that rewards a submissive and compliant feminine posture will actually contain more compliant and submissive women, due to habitual emphasis on the element of compliance and submissiveness in the individual woman. As between the sexes, however, this process is only a matter of degree. The women D and X on p. 33 are obliged to move 5 points along the adjustment scale, whereas the men E and

Y only move 3 points – but all must adjust. Nor is there any outright change in the individual posture profile, but only adjustment, since moving 5 points still makes X's score only 5 for compliance and submission, making her half rebellious and half compliant, whereas D, moving 5 points, becomes totally compliant. D does not, and cannot, become X, nor E become Y. Each twig, however harshly dragged from its natural growth, remains its own twig, so to speak, and everything previously discussed about adjustment and change remains true for both sexes.

All the same, the power of clothes to assist the individual in moving further towards conformity explains the continuous preoccupation with what women, on whom the pressures to conformity are greatest, and to a lesser degree men, ought to wear. For instance, a man may not be permitted to dress as his 'betters' for fear that he should adopt their posture and be like them. This is the basis of the elaborate hierarchy of dress in some schools, particularly boys' public schools. Women are the victims, historically speaking, of sumptuary laws, the enforced dress usually emphasizing sexual status or sexual attitudes. Prostitutes in Venice in the fifteenth century were forced to wear garish clothes, not only to ensure their distinction from 'good' women, but also to ensure that they *actually remained* 'bad' women. In a non-permissive age, the tendency of such women to cross the line to become good wives and mothers, given the opportunity, produces, from the male viewpoint, an unwelcome increase in dependants, and a reduction of sexual opportunities. Similarly 'good' women must show that they *are* so by the nicest attention to conformist dress. If a woman wears a trouser suit a few months before it is the fashion, judges fling her from the courtroom; if she holds to the mini skirt a few months too long, she is dismissed from the town council.

A short story illustrates both the power of clothes to assist in posture adjustment, and also the possibility of adjustment, but not change, in innate characteristics. A young man was utterly at a loss when estimating his girlfriend's innate characteristics, because of her chameleon-like ability to adjust to suit her clothes. Dressed in jeans, she was boyish and companionable; in furs, an elegant lady; in velvet cat-suit, a sex kitten; in a bikini, a nature girl. Unable to decide whether, or indeed who, to marry, he phoned her one night and asked her to talk to him with no clothes on. Shrewishly she told him off, saying that she already had nothing on as she had been getting into the bath, and sharply ordered him to wait while she turned the taps off.

He did not like her tone, but when she returned, such mellow and honeyed accents, such luscious graciousness, flowed over the wire, that he put her initial snappishness down to surprise, and proposed on the spot. Some weeks later, however, the shrewish nature of his new wife on their honeymoon re-awakened his suspicions, and he anxiously asked her whether, on the night of his proposal, she had in fact talked to him in the nude. She replied that she had until she went to turn off the bath taps, but on the way back had caught up the beautiful negligée with the expensive embroidery and the ostrich plumed collar, which had been a rich uncle's birthday present, and

now formed part of her trousseau, and which didn't 'count' as clothes. 'You didn't expect me to catch my death did you?' she snapped, adding with pride that the gown was 'fit for a queen'. Then her husband knew beyond doubt that he had married the shrew!

The generation gap

Since posture is partly determined by the conventional postural norms, and since these change from generation to generation, while adjustment to them does not change, it is easy to understand how postural expression widens the generation gap before young or old open their mouths. Regardless of *what* father and mother may *say* to son and daughter, they are already in communication, and out of sympathy, through their movement. They are unconsciously using the silent language of posture, and since each generation has used the postural range of adjustment to move closer to the conventional requirement of their own time, as best they may, their posture profiles are likely to be different. It is here that XYZ may score, if the younger generation now adopt, as desirable, postural conventions which in XYZ's generation were undesirable. They may obtain approval from the young that they could not gain from contemporaries, while ABC lose out. Figures 3.4, 3.5 and 3.6 illustrate the result of a reversal of the conventional requirement.

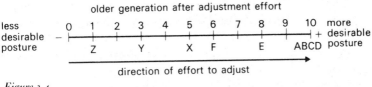

Figure 3.4

On the scale shown in Figure 3.4 the adjustment effort of nine individuals resulted in the distribution shown above. The continued efforts achieved a bunching at the top end of the scale and a total score of 63 points. However, if the conventional requirements are now reversed (so that the plus and minus change places as in Figure 3.5), the new generation will exert their efforts in the opposite direction, achieving only 27 on the older generation's scale but 63 if the scale be revalued to suit the new convention.

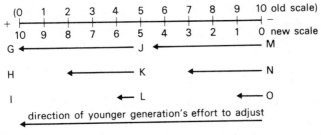

Figure 3.5

And since, in spite of the inevitable resistance of the older generation, the new conventional norm must supersede the old, the new distribution of the generations is as shown in Figure 3.6.

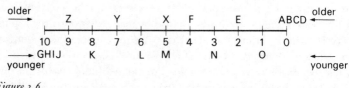

Figure 3.6

The older generation now scores 27 whereas the younger generation scores 63. Older conformists now score low, and deviants acquire acceptability. Generally speaking, however, since successful conformist adjustment is the rule, and such modifications become habitual, the posture profiles of the generations will differ, as shown in Figure 3.5 and where the old and the young predominate at opposite extremes of the scale.

For one generation to adopt the style of the other is almost impossible. Mother and daughter both wear jeans, and, wherever the mother shops, she may notice people lounging casually; yet it will be almost impossible for her to sit and stand like her daughter, because she has the habitual posture of the mermaid, derived from an upbringing suitable to a lady and a skirt, and not designed for the unashamedly bifurcated animal. Similarly, father brought up to adopt the spruce appearance and determined air of a generation, reared in war-time, and set adrift in the cold comfort of post-war austerity to rebuild the world, will never acquire the gentle almost lackadaisical charm of a generation brought up to full employment, peace and plenty. As we have already determined, postural habits rarely change once they are entrenched.

Posture in its place

We can now single out the determinants of posture:

1 The capacity of the individual to adjust his posture, that is to say his *range of postural adjustment*.

2 The influence of the changes in meaning given to posture and the degree of approval given to them in any society at any period, that is to say the requirements of *the conventional postural norm*.

It is in this sense that we *have* a posture. On the one hand it is individually characteristic, and depends on the range of postural adjustment of which we are capable, and, on the other, it is the product of habitual adjustment to the conventions of the society in which we live. Because there is a built-in adjustment range which varies with the individual, a posture profile can be modified; because the adjustment range, which varies with the individual, is none the less limited, and because the continuous adjustment that is made to meet social demands produce an ingrained habit, the posture profile cannot be changed outright. It can be shown as in Figure 3.7.

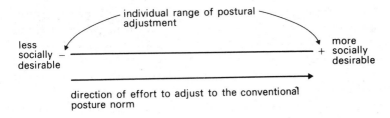

Figure 3.7

This, then, is the place of posture, but of course it is never fixed in its place for a moment!

4

Posture pattern

There is no such thing as a fixed posture in real life, any more than there is a static wave. If it were stilled, it would be a miracle of ice, or a marine painting, but not a wave, just as a fixed posture applies to a statue or portrait, or a corpse, but not to a living person. You can describe the nature of a wave, saying that the waves today are smooth, or unbroken, or fierce, or lumpy, or foamy, or what you will, but the wave is always in movement, endlessly variable. As you can speak of the characteristics of a wave, so you can speak of a natural, habitual posture, or posture profile, and describe it. We have already done this in the previous chapter. But in a sense, this is misleading, because it suggests that you *can* catch a wave and pin it down, that you *can* fix posture in its place, whereas in reality, a wave is, so to speak, always waving, and a posture is always posturing. No sooner has a wave risen from the ocean bed, than it is heaving up, peaking, breaking, and withdrawing, and no sooner has posture expressed itself in one form, than it is varied to another. The simple fact that we live to move, is the basis of many children's games, particularly the one variously known as 'Attitudes', or 'Statues', or 'Shapes'. Someone stops the music and cries out 'Napoleon' or whatever attitude takes his fancy, and everyone adopts a Napoleonic posture, and waits breathlessly for a player to shift his position. Needless to say, it is all over in moments! Someone goes 'out' for varying his posture a second ahead of the inevitable moment when all the competitors would have been forced to vary theirs. Stand like Napoleon yourself, and you will find that before long, you must vary this attitude, because like the wave we are always in motion, however slightly.

It is, then, more empirically correct to say that we have a characteristic *range of posturing*, rather than to continue to consider the nature of our posture profile. It is as though we have been holding a film motionless so that we can examine the nature of film, but can now let the reel continue. A film that is not in motion is not experienced as a film, and since to live is to move, a person in a fixed posture is not alive.

Just as a film is a continuous flow of photographic impressions, so a posture profile expresses itself continuously in variable, but characteristic, body movements. We can describe this as its characteristic range of posturing, or, more succinctly, as its *posture pattern*. A posture pattern is a posture profile in movement or posturing. We are releasing our 'hold' on posture, as we release it on a film, so that we can look for the meaning of postural expression in bodily movement. The secrets of the meaning are in the movement, that is to say in the range of posturing or the posture pattern of each individual. We can say: a posture profile expresses itself in posturing or movement. It has a characteristic *range of posturing*, or *posture pattern*. We can visualize it with a drawing, Figure 4.1, which illustrates posture profile once again.

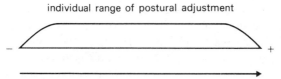

individual range of postural adjustment

direction of effort to adjust to the conventional posture norm

Figure 4.1

This time, however, we shall not consider it as a fixed phenomenon but set it in motion so that, as it spins like the hand of a clock, it can describe posture pattern for us. Our posture pattern will then look like Figure 4.2.

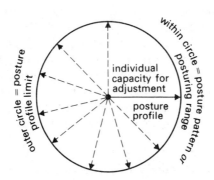

within circle = posture pattern or posturing range

outer circle = posture profile limit

individual capacity for adjustment

posture profile

Figure 4.2

You can see at once from this drawing that the range of posturing or the posture pattern lies within the limits of the posture profile, and those limits depend on the individual capacity for posture adjustment. This is only to say that I cannot move like you, or you like me, because we have individual posture profiles, any more than a dog can move like a tortoise.

The meaning of posture pattern: interpretation

Every individual's posture pattern is unique, and conforms to his individual posture profile. It is quite different from any other person's posture profile – as different as my fingerprints from yours. Although it will have certain traits in common with other patterns in the same generation, due to similar social conditioning – whereby the women are mermaids or 'all over the place', and the men are ramrods or 'at ease' – it is particular to the individual and has a secret language of its own, with a meaning that, with the use of disciplined expertise, and suitable tools, can be 'read'. Even without expertise or tools, which presuppose both training and capital outlay on equipment, an aware-ness of the nature of body language can be developed to the point where understanding its meaning is much easier than it was before. Very few of us are at a complete loss if we have to make do without the ideal range of tools or skills in other fields, so we are likely to start out quite well as interpreters of the secret language, especially as we have one very important advantage. Whereas ordinary language can be very deceptive, and a person can 'lie like a trooper', or 'lie in his teeth', or 'lie in his beard', the language which does not come from the tongue, but from the whole body is, generally speaking, the soul of truth. Movement does not lie, and movement is compounded of posture and gesture. Gestures may be contrived, but contrived posture requires such a degree of conscious effort, that it is only produced on occasions of exceptional stress where the person is 'put on the spot', such as interviews, or public appearances, and the like. By and large, in everyday situations, we get a true reading from posture.

Familiarity in interpretation

Under certain circumstances, this reading is easily obtained, and the meaning of a posture pattern instinctively understood. This happens with the people who are very well known to us, or with whom we are in daily contact. Among people who make up a household, each person's posture pattern is so familiar to the rest, that interpretation is almost instantaneous. Look in on two similar households at the end of the working day, and see how this works! Sixth-formers Paul and Brian walk home together after an exam. Each walks in on his own family with the same posture. Paul's family glance at him, and read his movements correctly as 'pleased with himself'. Brian's family read identical movements – equally correctly – as 'making the best of a bad job'. The same movements 'tell' different stories to those familiar with the boys' posture patterns. Paul's mother will know, from her husband's entry, that *her* spouse will be a millionaire shortly and counts on immediate promotion, while next door's husband, entering in a similar manner, will be rightly interpreted by *his* wife as about to announce impending bankruptcy and ruin. Again similar postures 'tell' different stories to the initiated. As Paul's mother reaches for the teapot, the family interpret her movements as 'got it made', whereas Brian's family accurately interpret similar movements made by their unfortunate angel as 'needs brandy, not a cuppa'. The similar movements in the two households mean different things; *the meaning varies with the individual posture patterns.* It is successfully interpreted by the families concerned *because these are familiar.* In the language of Paul's posture pattern, a breezy homecoming means elation, whereas in Brian's it means defiance. Both fathers enter in a calm unhurried manner, but this means suppressed excitement in Paul's father, and blank despair in Brian's. The mothers are equally flurried – or sedate – but Paul's mother is cock-a-hoop, and Brian's at the end of her tether. Either way, the families 'get the message' without a word spoken, showing a real expertise in interpretation, which they would not have if a stranger were to walk in on them.

How is this expertise acquired? What is it that allows us to understand the secret language of someone we know well, while the stranger remains an enigma? Why should this expertise be so limited? Isn't it simply that with people we know well, we have *learned to perceive their posture patterns*, and have unconsciously built up a code of evaluation by which to interpret them? We are clued-up on the posture patterns of our family and friends, so that we understand them 'without a word spoken', whereas we do not know the posture pattern of the stranger, and so we cannot interpret his body language.

Since we are seeking a universal method of interpretation for the silent language, it is obvious that we cannot rely on a getting-to-know-you technique. In fact, it doesn't bear thinking about! How many people can we possibly live with, or frequently bump into, without screaming for a hermitage, a cell, a cave, or a deserted island? Even in communes, or institutions, or among crowds of students, actual contact between people is limited. Being 'alone in a crowd' may sometimes feel lonely, but being on familiar terms with large numbers of people would ruin our mental and physical health altogether. The 'familiarity' method can only be applied on a very limited scale. Another method must be found for the interpretation of posture patterns in general, and since these comprise a range of postures, it would seem logical to pick on postures for examination, in the hope that a closer look at the components of posture patterns will tell us more about the pattern itself. A study of the range of postures that we see every day, in casual encounters, may help us to 'read' the silent language of movement that goes on all around us.

Picking out postures

Consider what happens when you meet a stranger. Naturally enough, you want to know whether this person is threatening, aggressive, sympathetic, helpful or deceptive. How can you tell from the posture of someone who stops you to ask the way whether he is lost, or has designs on your wallet? Many people would explain that the stranger was clearly late for tea with a favourite aunt, because he 'looked them right between the eyes', or alternatively that, with such a shifty gaze, he was patently up to no good. But this snap judgment does not allow for the wallet-pinching ruffian who has purposely practised looking you in the eye, or for the self-conscious soul of honour, who never yet deceived anyone – not even the favourite aunt that he *is* going to see, although he cannot look you eyeball to eyeball as he says so! It is apparent that a 'looking you in the eye' posture, or a shifty one does not provide adequate evidence for reading meaning.

Meanwhile, your own postures at this meeting have been reflecting your thoughts, and these depend on your disposition, and the way you happen to be feeling. If you are generally a friendly person, and the day's events have convinced you that all is for the best in the best of all possible worlds, you will be 'reading' the stranger as a shy arch-visitor

of aunts, and doing your best to encourage his questions. If you have had a day when everything has gone wrong with you, you may give a curt answer, and hurry on clutching your wallet surreptitiously. If you are habitually unfriendly and suspicious, and you had felt, or been, put upon all day, you may decide that you have met the arch-deceiver himself, refuse to answer his query, clutch your wallet, and look for the law. Whatever your reaction, there will be two sets of postures, your own and the stranger's, and these will interact on each other, so that the stranger's posture will be affected by your own attitude. When you are trying to 'read' posture you have to make allowances for this interaction. This interaction would become much more obvious, if we could cut out words from the encounter, as is possible if it is filmed, and then run silently. The encounter then appears as a sort of dance, much of it made up of gesture of course, but with the postures telling the story of the meeting.

The *paramount importance* of posture in bodily expression is easily tested. Suppose we borrow from the Romeo and Juliet story, and create a condensed dramatic script. Romeo meets Juliet, it's love at first sight, they discover the family feud that divides them and (to give it a fatally commonsensical and unshakespearian twist) they both decide to seek other more suitable partners. We now ask two actors to

undertake the parts, with the proviso that the whole script must be conveyed in the silent language. If we also specify that *only gestures may be used*, and postures must be excluded, they will rightly tear the script across, and dive for the exit, because no actor, however talented, could get this theme across by gesture alone, unless there already existed, as in some Oriental theatre, an established and formal system of mime, whereby certain gestures were understood by the audience to carry a wider significance than they could do in their own right. However, if we were to specify 'posture only', the actors would get on with the job. A start of surprised recognition, some getting-together movements, some hand-clasping, an embrace, a backward start, hand to brow, tearing of hair and shaking shoulders, some eye-wiping and a resigned wave or two, and that would be that. Romeo and Juliet conveyed in posture!

Well almost! – if we had no clue at all to the subject or the environment of this scene, our understanding of the theme that was being communicated in the silent language might go badly astray. We might, perhaps, assume that the actors were in a hospital and were doctors and nurse. If so, we might conclude that they were congratulating each other on the success of their treatment, but suddenly realized that the patient had died after all, and were forced to part, swearing never to work together again. Similarly, if we were under the impression that Romeo and Juliet were meeting at a party, when in fact the meeting was in the graveyard, we would be utterly baffled by the postures, and fail to 'read' their meaning.

Posture interpretation – the proper method

From this study of posture, we can see that every encounter is made up of a blend of posturing, which makes it appear like a form of dance. The quality of the movement is continually varied, and the participants start off with one attitude, and leave with another. These postures can be observed, filmed and, using a disciplined set of terms, recorded. It is apparent that each person does not have one posture, but an individual posture pattern, which can be discovered, and noted down. In this way different posture patterns can be isolated, and the difference between them examined. This allows us to apply universally, the methods that we already use instinctively within our families and 'familiarity' circle. We have seen that we are best placed to interpret posture pattern if we know the person concerned, understand our interaction with him, and are aware of the context of environment in which this movement takes place. However we cannot rely on this, but must practise drawing the shape of posture patterns from our own observation. In the illustration on page 43, we have drawn this shape as a circle to formalize the idea. But in fact each individual range of postures or posture pattern has its own distinct shape. All that has been said of the circle remains true, but it does not have a hard edge. It has a flexible one, which different people shape differently. The way they posture makes a pattern round which you can draw a particular envelope. It is only a circle *in theory*.

Sculpture in posture: the shape of posture patterns

Throughout our waking life, and even asleep in bed, we vary our postural position. The actual process of variation, which results in a succession of differently sculpted positions, can be described as a *sculpturing*, or *shaping process*. If we wish to become more aware of the shape of a person's posture pattern, as he dresses himself, or greets friends at a party, or elbows his way around a store, for example, it helps to imagine that all his joints are emitting vapour trails as though they contained jet engines. In this way, his movements become visible and he creates a plethora of vapour trails around himself, similar to the trails that aircraft leave behind them in the sky, but, in this case, confined within the space surrounding the body. Although the trails criss-cross and seem muddled at first, they create an individual and distinctive shape around him, and make us aware of the actual process of posture-shaping.

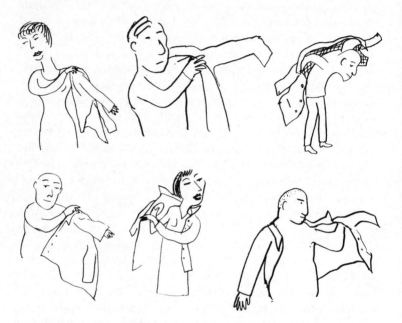

Watch how a group of people put on their coats, when it is time to go home. Everyone performs this simple action differently! Some appear to slide into their coats, others struggle belligerently, some throw them on casually, some wriggle in tentatively, and some fuss themselves in with meticulous attention to detail. Even a straightforward activity allows scope for wide variation in human behaviour; there are as many different ways of putting on a coat as there are owners. As we try to perceive the individual patterns in these differences, we must note not only the different postural positions which are adopted, but the actual pathways which each person's movement traces. One way of doing this is to imagine vapour trails, but another way would dispense with imagination and equip each person with lights on all his joints, so that a film could be taken that would show the actual path-ways followed by the active parts of the body. Film is often used in this way as an aid to industrial or sports training.

Whether we use film or imaginary vapour trails to heighten our awareness of posture shaping, we will not be surprised to find that the act of putting on a coat creates a considerable tangle of movement, although each person's tangle has a different form. Some simple geometry can help us to distinguish these forms.

When we move, we carry our space with us, 'our' space is the area in which we can extend our body and limbs, and is known as our kinesphere, or the space within which we move. You have only to swing your arms around you in all directions to become aware of the nature of this space. Clearly it is not a two dimensional circle, because you can reach out not only sideways, but also upwards and down-wards, forward and back. It has three dimensions, and is in fact a

sphere, and not some other three-dimensional geometric shape, such as a cube or a pyramid. Your kinesphere is a bubble in which you move. If you stand still to put on your coat, you have your kinesphere anchored as it were, whereas if you put it on as you walk away, your kinesphere-bubble goes with you. Whether anchored or in motion, the way in which movement is shaped within it can be described using a single set of terms.

How, then, is movement shaped within the kinesphere? We must begin by examining a simple action. Our choice of activities such as getting dressed, or even simply putting on a coat, may provide a useful illustration of the sculptural way in which we vary our postural movement, but creates too great a tangle of movement from which to extract posture shapes. It would be better to concentrate on a single reaching movement where posture is involved, because the distance is too far for the movement to be confined to a gesture of the arm alone. Here is an illustration of reaching in a *horizontal plane* so that the imaginary vapour trails left by the arm and shoulder are more or less parallel to the floor.

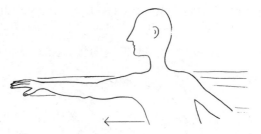

Try doing this. Make sure that the vapour trails are fairly parallel. Reach out as far as you can – the bigger the movement the more obvious its shape becomes. Imagine a hoop fixed horizontally around your waist, and your reaching movements aim to trace its circumference. You are now moving in a way technically called: enclosing–spreading.

If you reach out so as to sweep imaginary crumbs from a table and carry on until you have wrapped your arm around the body you will end up in a straitjacketed position. You cannot go any further until you change the movement – you are fully 'enclosed'.

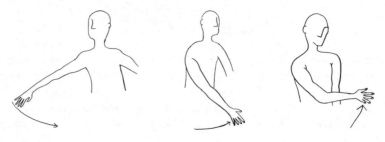

Now reverse the process and see what happens.

We call this 'spreading'. Obviously there is a limit beyond which you just cannot physically spread any more:

This looks rather like a pop star who was observed trying to spread himself more and more to his audience until it must have physically hurt him!

Between these extremes there is obviously a range of varying degrees. Some of us move habitually so as to look like these pictures more than others.

There are alternative ways of moving. Let us, for example, divide the kinesphere so that we imagine a *vertical plane*. The imaginary hoop is now upright around us. All our vapour trails are shaped so that they go up and down. Obviously there is a limit beyond which we can reach upwards or downwards.

Experiment by believing you are attracted by lofty thoughts in a heavenly direction:

Now with a deep sense of unworthiness you descend.

The extremes in this case are easily experienced. If you rise upwards, and you are not endowed with miraculous powers of levitation, you will reach a point beyond which you just cannot go any higher. Attempts to do so, in fact, cause you to reverse downwards to some degree. The descending movement also has its limits. Just as you have either to come down from the heights or to levitate at the extreme of the rising movement, so you have to reverse upwards or disappear through the floor at the limit of a descending movement.

As we consider the process of posture shaping in the horizontal and vertical planes, we must always remember the essentially sculptural, shaping nature of body movement. You can stick an arm upwards in the gesture signal for 'please may I leave the room?', familiar to every classroom, or you can stretch both arms above your head as you would at a keep-fit class, but these are symmetrical, dimensional, straight-up-and-down movements which, as it were, relatively squash and stretch the body, but do not change the shape other than in terms of elongation, much as Plasticine is lengthened or shortened by stretching or squeezing. If you compress a Jack-in-the-box under the lid, and then let him shoot out, you do not change his shape sculpturally. Symmetrical, dimensional movement anchors the centre of gravity, and restricts sculptural variation. If it didn't, then Jack would not fit back inside the rim of his box. With sculptural movement, we are venturing out into kinesphere, which is the space between us and the inner surface of the imaginary globe. It has to be a sphere or globe, and not a cube or any other shape, because all movements, extended to the physical limit, transcribe arcs, which together form a sphere. The only way you can transcribe a straight line continuously at the limit of your physical reach – a straight vapour trail if you prefer – is to stick your arm out as far as possible, and then travel as though you were running with an Olympic torch. Otherwise, to make a straight vapour trail, you have to come *inside* the sphere and chop off a segment.

Movement sculptured to the physical limits involves rounded, curving, arc-like, circular motions. Accordingly, the rising movement shapes itself along a curve which gives the maximum 'feel' of upwardness. Whereas a symmetrical lifting of the arms looks and feels robot-like, the sculpted, rising movement looks and feels as though you are drawing yourself up to your full height. It is the sort of movement which accompanies a haughty, 'What do you mean by that?' when someone has been outraged by some tactless remark. Similarly, someone who calls out 'idiot!' and bangs the table, using a straight up and down dimensional movement, will look, and feel, silly or petulant, whereas if the movement is shaped along a descending curve, there is a much greater chance that he will look impressively authoritative. Try these movements if you want to look outraged or authoritative. If you are not that sort of person, we can say in advance that you will have difficulty in shaping these rising and descending movements.

We have adopted a scheme for dividing the kinesphere into three zones, and so far we have considered two of these, the horizontally oriented and the vertically oriented. There is, of course, only one left – the forward–backward or, to borrow a medical term, the sagittally oriented.

Sagittal movement forward has an extreme when you are either forced to hop or fall on your nose. Similarly, the backward variation leads either to a hop or to bouncing with a bump on your bottom.

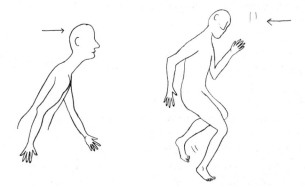

Have you ever had the experience of talking to someone who looks as though he is coming for you one minute, causing you involuntarily to edge backwards and then the next minute is retiring away from you, arriving at a sort of 'on your marks' ready for another advance? He is a sagittal mover!

We could use other schemes to divide up the kinesphere, but the one we have adopted has the merit of simplicity. We are simply saying that it is possible to shape our movement within three primary zones. Like planets moving into orbit around the sun, we can cause orbiting vapour trails around our own body centre through the way we shape our movement. We have described three main zones of shaping, each with limits, which can be described in Figure 4.3.

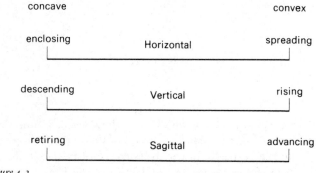

Figure 4.3

The first three produce a closed, concave shape; the second three an open convex shape. Between each extreme there is an infinite number of variations of degree. When we are observing other people's movement, we will find that some people's vapour trails tend more to one of the three zones than to the other two. Any such tendency has the effect of appearing to divide the kinesphere into two.

For example, horizontally oriented movement appears to be saying that there is a big distinction between the upper part of the body and the lower.

In the eighteenth century, European clothes, especially women's, encouraged this 'sculputral' effect and it was part of the social behaviour of the times that every part of the body above the waist was mentionable, everything below unmentionable.

The vertically oriented sculpturing has the effect of segregating all that is in front of the body from all that is behind. When we are in the presence of someone whose movement is vertically oriented we are in no doubt that he is facing us or has turned his back on us. With such people it always seems to be either one or the other. When he faces a group of people he seems to be marking out a territorial boundary.

Experiments with teachers and children have shown that a teacher

who sculptures vertically oriented movement while saying 'no one is to come past me',

is successful in getting the children to stay back. When the same statement is made by a teacher who sculptures horizontally oriented movement, children filter past. This teacher makes it seem that she is in touch with the environment all around her and she thereby makes it inviting.

Have you ever had the experience at a cocktail party of talking to someone who seems to be giving attention all round you, making it seem he is exploring around to see whether there might be someone more interesting to talk with than you? Such a person is sculpturing his movement on the spreading–enclosing (horizontally oriented) scale. In contrast, if you happen on to someone who is sculpturing his movement in the rising–descending scale (vertically oriented) you will be aware that you have got him, whether you like it or not, and he has turned his back on everyone else in the room.

The person who sculptures his movement in a forwards–backwards orientation has the effect of dividing left from right. Such movement has an ordering, organizing character. Groucho Marx, puffing his cigar, used to move in this way. It seemed as though he was wearing blinkers, heading first one way then another, carving up the environment into sections. Whether he actually succeeded in organizing anything is another matter. The teacher in the playground, however, sorting out children into different teams for some game, will achieve success more readily when his or her movement is predominantly sculptured in this way.

Similarly the hostess at a cocktail party will look much more as though she knows what she is doing, as though she has a plan, when she rushes around introducing people, using this type of movement.

Try yourself to see these different forms of shaping of movement in other people's behaviour. Sometimes it will be difficult because a lot of people do not make their sculpturing clear. Others may not use one of the three zones predominantly but sculpture in all three, i.e. the vapour trails look partly horizontal, partly vertical, partly sagittal, which gives a diagonal orientation. Nearly always, however, a person will show some *inclination* towards one or other of the zones.

Try also to vary your own movement in the ways indicated. The more you can involve the whole body, as distinct from an isolated arm gesture, the more will you get the feeling of what the varied sculpturing expresses. As a discipline for developing your perception it helps to use a simple scheme for recording your observations on paper. For example, the form of shaping in respect to each zone can be shown roughly as a line between the two extremes:

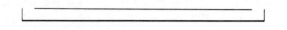

= a lot of movement from one extreme to the other.

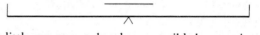

= a little movement, barely perceptible because it avoids both extremes where the shape distinctions are obviously most apparent.

= a little movement, but obviously apparent, because it is close to an extreme.

If we take each shaping component in turn we shall then categorize distinct personal styles in movement shaping behaviour:

(a)   1 The 'spreader'

— rather like the proverbial sower.

— with its extreme – the man so spread out he can hardly spread any more.

2 The 'encloser'

spreading   enclosing

— who looks as though he is constantly wrapping the space around himself.

— the extreme looks as though he has succeeded in straitjacket-ing himself.

(b)   1 The 'riser'

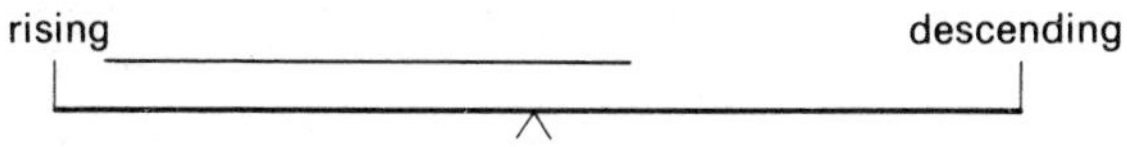

rising _____ descending

— with his head in the clouds.

— so stuck that he can hardly come down from his lofty regions.

2 The 'descender'

rising _____ descending

— very much down to earth.

— and now sunk to extreme depths, perhaps with little promise that he will ever rise out of them.

(c)   1 The 'advancer'

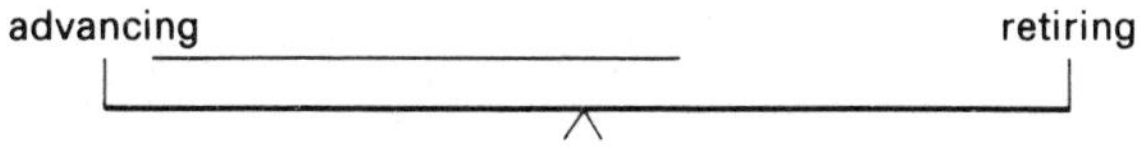

advancing _____ retiring

— so forward looking as to be almost coming out of his chair.

— and now ahead of himself – he cannot physically advance in his body shape any further.

2 The 'retirer'

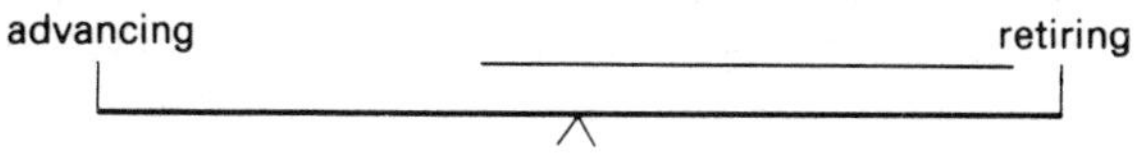

advancing _____ retiring

— seems to take the space back with him into the furthest reaches of his chair.

— and to have become so stuck he looks as though he will never emerge.

It is worth repeating again that such impressions derive from observation of a trend over a sequence of movement and we should not attempt to see one position corresponding to the above illustrations. We can indicate the sort of movement-shaping diagrammatically, so as to show what has actually happened to give these impressions:

(a)

As we see one spreading occur we can record it with a line in the appropriate direction:

(b)

When we see it reverse, we reverse the line as in (c).

(c)

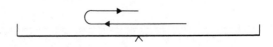

We try to judge how close to the extreme came the reversal. Eventually we have a series of lines. They will not be continuous because it is impossible to keep track of all the variations happening. It is, however, possible to see excerpts clearly and they should be shown as in (d).

(d)

spreading   enclosing

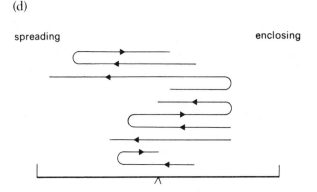

If this occurs more or less in isolation of the other components (a possible but unlikely occurrence) we have the *predominant* 'spreader'.

Where movement goes to the extreme, this is shown:

Our subject may, of course, include both spreading and enclosing in his repertoire of shaping movements and if we see this it could be recorded, as shown in the illustration above where a number of excerpts have been recorded.

Where this record is shown, the subject is still a predominant 'spreader', though not so marked as is possible. We could analyse all the recordings and show the result as a single line indicating the range covered:

spreading   enclosing

— which gives us some idea of how predominant a 'spreader' the subject is.

Of course, our subject is 'playing' in all three shaping components simultaneously. We therefore need to try and record all the variations we see during the phrase which has been selected for observation. It is obviously impossible for anyone to observe every movement. When a phrase is selected, however, it should be observed and recorded in complete detail, such as (a):

(a)

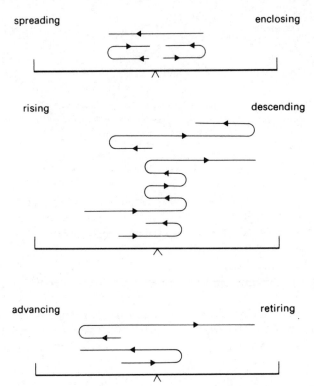

spreading   enclosing

rising   descending

advancing   retiring

Here we see a predominant 'descender', but we are able to appreciate his predominance relative to other components. Analysis of recordings could be diagrammatically shown (b):

(b)

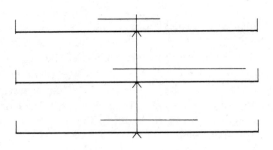

or rounded off for compactness as (c):

(c)

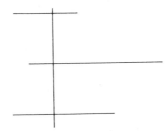

Extracted in this way (assuming the observations are both accurate and representative of the subject's behaviour) we have a simple diagrammatic expression of how a person shapes his physical movement behaviour.

We have, in fact, been able to devise a way of pinning down our wave which is never still for a moment. We can now observe the pattern of movement made by any individual and analyse it, drawing down the shape of movement in a definite posture pattern. The more practised we are at doing this the more accurate our basis for an interpretation of movement behaviour will be, so we should make as many movement sculptures as possible from our observations of family, friends and colleagues. This will help us to a firm foundation for efforts at interpretation of the speaking silence.

However postures always have gestures going on around them, and with voluble, demonstrative people, they act like a smoke-screen obscuring posture. Posture pattern has taken us a long way towards interpreting the secret language. If we can now discover a gesture pattern as well, and investigate its relation to posture pattern, we shall have yet another dimension to work on. Together posturing and gesturing make up the process of movement. Perhaps it is in the complete process of movement that the meaning of body language can be found.

5
The meaning is in the movement

The kinaesthetic sense

You may think that the meaning of body language is something that you, for one, interpret quite naturally. You can 'tell at a glance', 'know just by looking at him', 'see just by looking at her', that he or she is honest, flighty, feckless, hardworking or whatever, and you may take it for granted that others have this ability too. If so, you will be one of those who are hurt, or angry, or irritated if a prospective employer makes a fuss about references for a casual job. 'If he can't tell by looking at me,' you mutter, as you move on to look for someone more perceptive.

Now you may well be right! – right for you that is, though quite wrong to expect everyone to be like yourself. It is possible that you are one of those people who have a natural flair for judging others from the language of movement. Experiments have shown that some people are consistently more accurate than others in making judgments based on non-verbal behaviour. Such people instinctively describe others as though they had seen them on film, rather than in a snapshot, using words such as:

Creep	Slow-coach	Wanderer
Twister	Drifter	Gad-about
Fire-eater	Pace-setter	Smooth-operator
Bounder	Ball-of-fire	Speed merchant
High-flyer	No-hoper	Cock-a-hoop
Go-getter	Flighty	Fusspot
Stay-at-home	Sleep-walker	Heavy-breather
Globe-trotter	Dozy	Lightweight

These words describe manner, and you can only assess manner from film, which shows movement. A photo, which shows appearance, does not give you any idea whether someone is quick, slow, lazy, calm, hesitant, gentle, keen, enthusiastic, abrupt and so on. From a photo, you can describe someone as attractive, dignified, slight, fat, tall, pompous, handsome, or imposing, but you can only judge how they look. You cannot tell how they might behave.

The fact is that people to whom the silent language of movement speaks so clearly, as it may do to you, have minds that take 'movies' rather than 'snaps', so that for them encounters are recorded on mental film, and not on mental transparencies. If they recall a meeting, they do not get a flashback to a static image, but a playback of the move-ment, which their particular mental cameras have recorded. These people have a natural kinaesthetic sense; or feel for movement, which is much more highly developed than usual, so that without effort or training, they note manner and behaviour and are aware of the silent language of the body. But for others this is much more difficult, since their mental cameras are instamatic, and record a series of appearance in static images. Fortunately, although we cannot take photos which are less and less static, and more and more movie, but have to settle for whichever type of camera we happen to possess, we can become gradually more and more aware of movement, or non-verbal behav-iour, judging it with more accuracy as we grow more perceptive. We are all perceptive to some degree! No one is so under-developed in kinaesthetic sense that he cannot discern some distinctions in the process of movement, and everyone can build on this foundation, to achieve a new level of kinaesthetic awareness.

All the same, it is hardly surprising that most research into non-verbal behaviour has been carried out in static terms, rather than in terms of movement, since the majority of us start out with mental instamatics and static images, and the people with the kinaesthetic gifts and the movie minds are in short supply. You can see this tendency to exclude movement very clearly in accounts of research into eye contact and body proximity. In these studies, the duration of eye contact between two people during an encounter has been timed with a stop-watch, revealing significant differences between indivi-duals especially of different nationalities, but *how* the eyes were moved, or the degree to which other parts of the body were involved is not recorded. Because the studies do not comprehend movement, we do not know whether the eyes moved quickly or slowly as they made contact, or whether their movement was supplemented by another, such as an inclination of the head. Similarly, the distance at which people come to rest when talking to each other has been efficiently measured and recorded, showing, for example, that Arabs tend to stand closer to each other than the British or the Americans do in similar circumstances, but, once again, the movement is missing, so that we learn nothing of the different ways in which such peoples approach each other. If we ask the more interesting questions which begin, 'in what manner . . .', we find there is no answer. What we really need to know is not how much, but simply *how*, because although there is a limited amount of useful knowledge obtainable from the static image, the real meaning is in the movement, and further useful data can only be obtained from an analysis of movement itself.

It is, of course, extremely difficult to get at movement for the purpose of disciplined study. Taking a film is an obvious first step, since filmed movement can be speeded up, slowed down, or replayed, and is generally more available for analysis than the movement in the raw of everyday life, but it is only a first step, because some way also has to be found of noting and recording what happens. If you are asked to observe and describe someone's movement, you will appreciate that this is more difficult than it sounds. Nothing happens – or everything happens at once. Movement is as slippery as an eel, and before it can be properly recorded or pinned down, it is gone, leaving the observer hot and bothered. It is as though you were asked to record the onrush of a wave to the shore. Could you say for certain where it formed, just how long it lasted before it broke, and describe the manner of its disappearance? It would be so much easier to enjoy the movement on a surf-board, than to record and analyse it! However, techniques for training movement observation do exist, and kinaesthetic sense can be systematically developed, in spite of the difficulties. They cannot be fully mastered through this book alone, because that would be like trying to acquire an appreciation of music without hearing any, but a very useful beginning can be made by learning to differentiate between the components of movement – posturing and gesturing.

Posturing and gesturing in detail

Suppose you decide to examine a simple posturing–gesturing movement that anyone can visualize, or see in any library? Equipped with a movie camera, you arrive at the nearest scene of reading or research, and sure enough within moments, someone strokes his chin. You record this movement, wait for a second example, which comes as someone else consults a directory, and leave with both movements on film to examine and interpret chin stroking at leisure. If this goes to plan, you can make useful movement-observations. Imagine, however, that you were called away from the library before you could film these movements, and had to leave the job to a friend with an instamatic camera. He loyally produces two portrait photos for you, but these prove sadly inadequate for interpretation. Both photos show men with chins lightly gripped between thumb and fingers, and the two positions look more or less identical. You cannot visualize the action in relation to the facial expressions, bodily stance, or immediate environment. You cannot tell *how* the movement was performed, and so you have nothing to go on.

As it happens, the two movements were performed very differently. The first man was sitting down at a table with his hand resting on it as the movement began. He lifted it with a quick jerk, twisted it slowly towards his chin, which he gripped strongly as the camera clicked. The second man was standing up, with his hand hanging at his side, and he lightly and slowly extended his arm outwards before in one quick sweep he seized his chin, and came to rest for his

unexpected portrait. It will, however, almost certainly be quite useless to apply to your friend for this vital extra detail. Like the rest of us, he will find it dificult to recall the actual process of movement, although he will instinctively have reacted to it. If pressed, he will probably tell you that the first man seemed tense and irritable, whereas the second was serene but dubious, giving you his snap interpretation of the movement, rather than a description of it. He will jump from observation to interpretation, without recording the movement, which is hardly surprising since he has no 'language' of movement with which to record it. However, if we are to exercise perception in interpreting movement, some method of recording it must be found.

Fortunately, notations do exist which allow an observer to record posture and gesture movement in detail as it happens, and although practice is needed to use observation techniques and notation skilfully, some people have a natural aptitude in this direction. There is also a great deal of assistance available from gadgetry! The use of film has already been discussed and, as we have seen, the inarticulate friend's inadequacies were compounded by his want of a movie camera. For the professional researcher, electromyography offers great scope, because it records muscle-movement in various parts of the body with a detail, continuity and accuracy impossible to the human eye. It is to be hoped that the appalling scenarios which inspire science fiction writers are never translated into reality. If, however, the entire population were struck deaf, dumb and blind at once, the only means of communication would be through the language of movement. Since we would be unable to see this movement we should be forced to move around permanently equipped with electrodes, together with miniature receiver and transmitter, judging the behaviour of others from the signals given – always supposing that such equipment could be supplied and maintained from elsewhere! Meanwhile, in more normal situations, the use of electromyography can tell us whether our attempts to observe movement are on the right lines. An electromyographic record of the chin-stroking gesture we have been already trying to examine, could well show variations in pace, direction and pressure, all within one or two seconds of movement. Obviously such a record provides much more data than a photo of a fixed or rest position, or even a film sequence, and its analysis yields all sorts of interesting results, sometimes contradicting the conventional interpretation of gesture, which in this instance would assert: chin-stroking = careful consideration.

Far from supporting this interpretation, a record of the movement might suggest that the gesture expressed satisfaction, doubt, boredom or a thousand and one other meanings – not to mention the possibility that the subject was assessing his need for a shave by the prickle of bristle. This only goes to show that as soon as we attempt to attribute meaning to movement, we are up to the neck in problems, even if our chins pass every test, or present no problems in the first place! For instance, if we accept the conventional interpretation of chin-stroking, what do we mean by 'careful consideration'? Are we assessing the feelings of the subject, or the effect the gesture has on us as onlookers? Does the chin-stroker actually feel carefully considerate, and also convey this to us, or does he convey it without feeling anything of the sort, either deliberately or by chance? Then again, we must carefully consider how far chin-stroking may be characteristic of this or that person, or liable to be provoked by a particular situation. Before we can give a meaning to a specific gesture, we have to have some record which gives a basis for comparison. We need to know of the hundreds of different ways in which chins are stroked!

Film is invaluable for this purpose, because it allows detailed analysis of a few seconds of movement, where a fixed position is quickly exhausted as material for study. A film producer may include an occasional still for effect, but it can only be held momentarily without provoking an impatient reaction from the audience. On film, as in life, the meaning is in the movement, and for this reason it is meaningless to refer to 'a posture' or 'a gesture' when trying to understand behaviour. We are forced to speak of posturing and gesturing to be accurate, but, since these are clumsy terms, we would do well to agree that 'posture' and 'gesture' shall, from now on, indicate a phrase or sequence of actions, rather than a single action, so that we can examine movement as a sequence of actions, each one following continuously from its predecessor, as one wave follows another to the shore.

Movement as a sequence of actions

To return to your friend in the café near the library where you have been examining his unhelpful portraits! You have been sitting there relaxing over a cup of cofee, but now you give a start. Try this out in ham-acting, and you will see that this involves an upward jerk, after which single postural movement, you remain frozen in your seat. Your friend, ever-hasty with interpretations, does not ask, 'What's up?', but starts guessing. 'Forgotten something?', he asks, or 'Are you ill?', or, if he thinks you are given to seeing things, 'Not another spook?'. Of course, all these are possible interpretations of a sudden starting movement but there are also many others. Your friend's

choice will depend on his own predisposition. If he is forgetful himself, he will try the first question, if a hypochondriac, the second, and if ghost-hunting is his hobby, the third, and so on.

Other considerations may also influence him. He may know the sort of start you make when you have forgotten something, and his 'What is it this time?' may have a note of weary resignation, or the environment may influence him, as it would if the café were known to be haunted, or you may have been getting greener for the last half-hour, so that he was already wondering if you were going to be sick. At this point, in any event, his guesses are bound to be rather wild, since he has had so little to go on. You are still frozen in post-start position, and all he has seen is that single sharp upwards movement. But this is not the end of it! You cannot remain as though turned to stone indefinitely, and so something else inevitably follows on. What follows tells much more. If you slump drearily, he will feel more and more certain that once again you have left your keys behind; if your original start is followed by a whole succession of quick frightened movements, he will conclude that the café lives up to its reputation; if you follow on with a strong, twisting, gripping movement, he may settle for food-poisoning diagnosis. As soon as the movement is developed as a sequence of actions, a wealth of possible meaning is revealed. Your friend's original guess is confirmed or corrected, because this action-sequence combines (in a particular way) certain components which were not present in the original single action.

You can see at once that the components of an action-sequence appropriate to food-poisoning, would differ fundamentally from those appropriate to a haunting or a lock-out. The timing for instance would

vary. There would be a slow subsiding after the original sudden start, if you were resigning yourself to the absence of keys, or there would be an onset of even quicker action if the ghostly horde advanced further. This action might develop as a series of machine gun starts, which were not only rapid, but also in varied directions, while increasing sickness might lead to increased movement-pressure as the agony worsened. Here, then, you have three components of movement – timing, direction, and pressure – which may be combined in an infinite number of ways, and simply to know that they exist and to practise looking out for them can enhance your perceptivity, even before we set out to classify them.

We are more aware of body movement as soon as we recognize that:
1 Postures and gestures make up movement.
2 Movement is action-sequence with varying components.

Making an effort

The components of action-sequences occur because we make them happen by making an effort. We may not do this consciously. Even asleep we make efforts – you probably know whether you give, or get, the kicks! Only in coma can it be said that we make no effort, any more than, in this state, we can sculpture our movement in the ways we described in the last chapter. Otherwise, awake or asleep, as we shape our movement within our kinesphere, we apply effort to obtain variation, so that the shaping process is partnered by the effort process. This means that we not only shape our movement in the horizontal movements of the one-arm bandit, or vertically like doors blocking off space, or like power-saws chopping into the environment, but we also do this shaping using variations of the three effort components, direction, timing and pressure. Our one-arm bandit grabs too far left of the prize, our door slams suddenly or swings slowly, and our saw bites harder. Clearly, we can no longer consider variation in our postural shape in isolation, but must relate it to the ways in which we make an effort. Shape and effort are the two processes by which we create movement and the relationship between them is important for our understanding of movement behaviour.

The application of effort to the shaping process does not mean that the more effort we apply, the more shape variation we get. You could vary the shape of your movement considerably, say from spreading to rising, while using very restrained pressure, as you might if you were doing yoga exercises. Or you could aim a ferocious and quite unrestrainedly forceful kick with only minimal variation in shaping. If you had been swinging back and forth in the sagittal plane, a kick would vary the effort but the movement would still be shaped in the same plane. There is no automatic correlation between effort variation and shaping variation, so that, in theory, there is no reason why any particular sort of effort should not be combined with any particular sort of shaping.

In practice, however, some sorts of effort work out best when applied to certain sorts of shaping. You can see this if you try out some combinations which do not work out well. If you try to change from a spreading to a rising movement using effort that is too forceful or hurried, you may end up on the floor! Or, if you are speechifying, and thump the table in front of you so emphatically that it collapses, then your shape will also collapse as you lose balance. In these two action-sequences you have related shape and effort, but without achieving harmony between the processes.

When you make an effort which seems in harmony with the shape of your movement, you can be said to have achieved effort–shape affinity. Without this harmony, your movements can be said to lack affinity, and will seem clumsy. It is as though you had been playing happy families in movement, and had got the members of different families mixed up. Now although we have to be guarded in labelling movements as clumsy, because what seems so to me, may not seem so to you, this does not mean that the concept of effort–shape affinity cannot be useful, any more than happy family cards become useless because, once in a while, someone prefers to sort them in an unusual way.

`Effort–shape affinity

You can establish the effort–shape relationships for yourself, by taking each shaping zone in turn, and seeing what sort of effort belongs to it. Many experiments have already been carried out to decide this, and if you do some of them you can check the results. For instance, it has been found that there is a link between direction in effort, and horizontal shaping, and that within this there are certain affinities. Can you discover these? Do a spreading–enclosing movement, reversing from one to the other so that all your body is involved. Follow this by pointing your finger at something using a posture movement, and ask yourself whether this effort goes best with a spreading, or with an enclosing shape. Most people find a natural affinity between the pointing, directing effort and the enclosing shape. Conversely they link a spreading shape with the opposite wiping away or indirect circling sort of effort. This is after all what you might expect, since, if

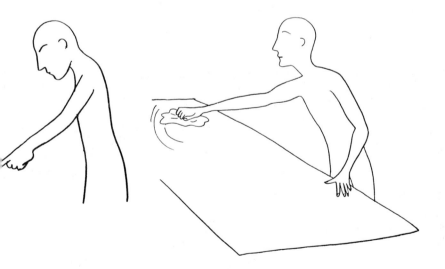

you want to confine attention to one point, the most helpful body action is one which encloses the space around you, shutting out distractions, whereas an indirect, circling effort spreads to the circumference of the horizontal zone.

If, when you carry out this experiment, you get a contrary result, this means that your behaviour pattern is atypical, and reverses the effort–shape relationship generally regarded as normal. It is as though you had sorted your happy family pack by fathers, mothers and children, and it is easier to say that this is unusual than to say it is good or bad. What we *can* say with confidence is that it does not bring the results you want, whether for playing the card game or for obtaining the most useful reaction from others through your body movements. You can check this next time you want to attract a friend's attention to something. Perhaps you are travelling by car and want him to see a rare bird, or a new type of plane, or an unusual shop. Your job is to direct your companion's attention to the object before you have passed on. If you spread your attention to him, but then enclose him in your pointing movement, you will probably succeed in sharing your experience before it is too late. If, however, you do not enclose him, but remain spread, shouting, 'Look', and staring at him as you point, he will not know whether to look at you, or in the direction of your finger, because you are applying energy in two directions and your movement is contradictory. Ten to one he will not share your experience at

all. An affinity movement produces the right reaction, and the other does not.

Of course, your success in directing a companion's attention depends not only on your movement affinity, but on his. If he lacks horizontal affinity you will not be successful in enclosing him, and you will feel frustrated, while he will view your behaviour with uneasy bafflement. Then again, you may be asking him to focus on something that he is conditioned not to notice, such as children, cream buns and wastebins, and be unsuccessful for this reason. However, this need not prevent us setting out as in Figure 5.1 the relationship between horizontal shaping and directing effort in the certainty that we have correctly established the affinities or links between them, and can cross off the non-affinities.

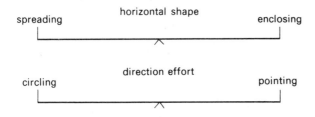

Figure 5.1

Just as horizontal shaping is related to direction, so shaping in the vertical plane relates to another effort-component – pressure. Rising and descending movements go with increase and decrease of pressure as surely as, at a party, bacon takes eggs in to supper, while knife partners fork. Try to shape your movements downwards, while pressing your weight more firmly into the floor, ending with an emphatic stamp as though to say, 'but you *must* . . . I insist!' This movement will probably seem quite natural and not at all ridiculous, whereas if you repeat the movement but lessen the pressure, to combine a descending shape with a flabby, lightweight effort, you will almost certainly look absurd. This is because your shaping and your effort are contradicting each other. It is more 'natural' to increase pressure downwards, by the same token that it is easier to press into the floor than into the ceiling! On the other hand, if you are speaking to a group and wish to gloss over a point tactfully, with a quite different emphasis to the stamping insistence with which you spoke earlier, most people would find that a rising shape with decreasing pressure would be the most natural manner to adopt. If you were to do the rising with increased pressure as you said 'we must consider all viewpoints . . .' or some such words, then the group would think you pompous, odd, or ill-at-ease. In this vertical plane then, the affinity is between rising shape and decreasing pressure, and between descending shape and increasing pressure. We can categorize vertical shaping and its related effort as in Figure 5.2, crossing off non-affinity in this zone.

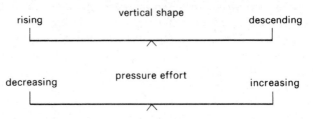

Figure 5.2

Again you can check the affinities we have decided on from the reactions to this type of movement. Experiments show that if there is affinity in the vertical zone, then others look to the person who is shaping his movement in this way expecting him to make a statement. This sort of vertical shaping happens when we draw ourselves up at

the airport to confess, 'I've forgotten my passport!' If we made this movement, but said nothing, our companion would still gather from our silent language that a statement was being made, and if he responded with affinity himself, it might not be necessary to use words at all. If he knew both you and the hazards of travel well, your movement might tell him what had happened. How often after all we can guess what someone is about to say before he speaks! Often he has told all in body language before he opens his mouth. On the other hand, non-affinity in vertical shaping causes a breakdown of the silent language, and the message that is received is not, 'This person wants to tell me something', but, 'This person is acting oddly'. Once again affinity in body movement proves more effective, if you judge by the reaction it brings. Our third shaping zone, the sagittal zone, in which back and forth movement occurs, is related to effort which varies pace or timing. This means getting faster or slower as you move. Again you can experiment for yourself to find the affinities.

Try accelerating both forwards and backwards. Does it come more easily as you lunge forward, or as you dart back? Probably you will agree with other experimenters that it comes more naturally as you shape your movement in a concave backwards way, and will have noticed that an athlete crouches in a retiring shape for a quick start, after which he decelerates slightly as he straightens out. It seems that the body is designed for accelerated withdrawal, probably as a protective mechanism. If you step into the road, and then dart back to escape

the traffic you can experience this quick withdrawal for yourself; the initial advancing into the road will come more naturally as a slowing movement – perhaps because there is inbuilt caution in advancing into the unknown.

If you now try out sagittal movements which lack affinity by combining backing with slowing, you will probably find that this has a defeated, giving-up quality to it, whereas acceleration in retiring feels as though you were simply preparing for a new advance. If you combine accelerating effort with advancing shape, this non-affinity movement gives an impression of impulsiveness often typical of teen-agers at the gauche stage, when they must screw up their courage for social entrances. So now in Figure 5.3 we can relate our final zone to the remaining effort-component, crossing off non-affinity.

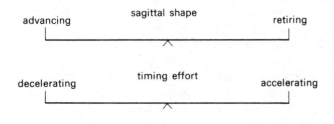

Figure 5.3

Once again the reactions to these different combinations tell us a great deal. If affinity movements are used in the sagittal zone, then other people either get a 'come on', message from the advancing–decelerating combination, or a 'let's get ready' message from the retiring–accelerating combination. Those with similar sagittal affinity will respond positively to these messages, whereas non-affinity move-ments in this plane tend to isolate the performer as though to say 'count me out!' Sadly, the silent language may convey this message through non-affinity, when the person desperately wants to be counted in. Non-affinity in movement brings frustration. Unfortu-nately, such contradictions between the silent language and what is consciously said or desired are legion. You cannot lay all the blame on non-affinity, because there are many other variables. However, it does help to be aware of contradictions in behaviour, and this should be easier now that we have categorized the relation between shape and effort, and examined the links or affinities between them.

The language of movement

Effort and shape are the two processes from which movement is created. In the last chapter, we devised a way of recording shaping behaviour using the horizontal, vertical and sagittal. We can now record the variations of effort in people's movement in exactly the same way, using the three effort categories which we have examined and related to their appropriate shaping zones in this chapter.

Just as we plotted on paper the extremes of shaping behaviour, showing the spreader and the encloser on the horizontal range, the riser and descender on the vertical range and the advancer and the retirer on the sagittal range, so we can now show different extremes of effort on the related directing, pressurizing and timing ranges. At the extremes of the direction range will be the person who goes indirectly to his objective, circling around it, while at the opposite end will be the man who goes straight to the point as directly as possible – perhaps someone who really is a company director because of his characteristic effort. Then on the pressure range there will be the person who has a lightweight, even flabby, quality in his movement and never pushes, but seems to give way gently, while at the other extreme there will be the real pusher so unpopular in shops, who uses his body in a firm resistant way. On the timing range, there will be the slow-coach, who always avoids hustle and bustle, and his opposite, the man shot from a gun.

When we have plotted these extremes of variation in effort behaviour, we can then examine and plot individual effort characteristics, using the same methods to record how near the effort came to the extremes as we used to record shaping, drawing down a diagram of the individual's effort behaviour on each of the three effort ranges. Finally, we can combine our findings from these three ranges to produce a diagrammatic expression of the sort of effort that a person characteristically employs in his movement, which we can lay beside the diagram we made in the last chapter of his shaping behaviour. This might give us diagrams like Figure 5.4.

Such diagrams show us the varying amounts of movement we have observed one person carry out. They tell us at a glance that here is a person who does not vary in advancing–retiring shape very much. He varies much more in spreading–enclosing. We also see that the spreading–enclosing is out of affinity with the circling–directing of effort. Diagrams like this, assuming that they represent a fair sample of the

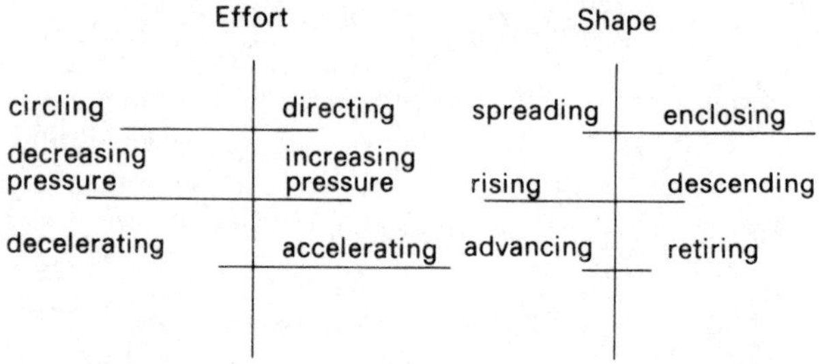

Effort		Shape	
circling	directing	spreading	enclosing
decreasing pressure	increasing pressure	rising	descending
decelerating	accelerating	advancing	retiring

Figure 5.4

person's movement, can tell us a lot.

We can build such diagrams by observing a person for some time and asking ourselves 'In what effort and shape do I see movement happening most?'. It will help if we keep in mind the six respective see-saw yardsticks. Perhaps a more useful model is to picture six spirit levels, each with a bubble which is always in a wavering state, but with some bubbles moving more than others at different times. It is not easy to chart the progress of six bubbles all in a constant state of movement, or potentially poised for movement. Diagrammatically it might look something like Figure 5.5.

If we plotted the movement bubbles in order to make the diagram it might look something like this. Of course the bubbles do not necess-arily move either continuously or simultaneously. They may all be held still. Then perhaps just one will move, then another join it. Or they could all be furiously in movement at the same time!

You are now setting shape and effort into the same language, recording it in the same way, so that you can see not only the shape of a person's behaviour, but also the manner in which it is shaped. It is this combination of carefully recorded shape with equally carefully re-corded effort that makes it possible for us to go on to give an interpreta-tion to a person's body movement. Although we pinned movement down by recording the shaping process, we found that we could not interpret it in this static form, but had to find a way of observing and recording the manner of the movement. The meaning of movement is to be found in the way in which the pattern changes or in the relation between shape and effort which we can now record, and analyse. We have in fact developed a language of movement, which puts the understanding of body movement within our reach, whereas before it could only be read by the unusual people with the movie minds, or the natural kinaesthetic talents.

Figure 5.5

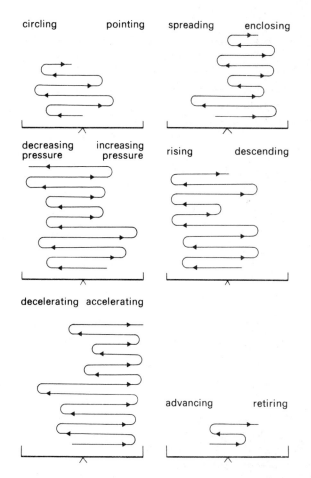

Indeed once we get the hang of this changing pattern of body movement, it is amazing not only how much more we can perceive, but also how the most simple action takes on new dimensions. Turning a page of this book will probably involve at least three or four actions, such as a slight hand-adjustment to bring the fingers in touch with the page, and a gripping, lifting, placing and releasing of it. All will require minute variations of timing, pressure and directions which different readers will phrase to suit themselves, one twisting the page, another stroking it, and another adding more finger actions because he cannot separate it, and even more if it will not lie flat.

If you are appalled to find so many components in this simple action, and take it out on the book, worse will follow. Down goes the book, and up you spring from the chair. But immediately your newly developing kinaesthetic sense comes into action, pointing out that there were several actions combined in what you planned as a quick dismissal. In the moment that it took to toss this book at the cat, you cannot help but notice the closing, lifting, aiming, and propelling of it, never mind the releasing of the fingers, and recovery of the arm, where

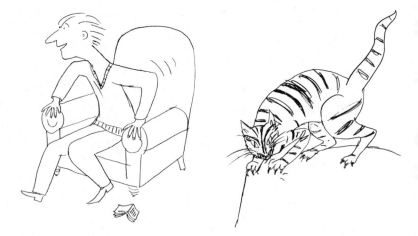

the cat now clings with tigerish revenge. Springing from the chair is even more complicated, with or without the domestic tiger. To rise a bare inch from a deep armchair involves gripping the arms, wriggling your weight forward, transferring this weight to each leg, and shifting it as you push on the arms, while every one of these actions causes the various components of movement to take place in different parts of the body with varying degrees of rhythmic synchronization. If this sounds complicated, it cannot be helped. Movement is complicated – but at least we have established that it can not only be observed, but also effectively recorded, using our new language of movement.

6

Posture–gesture merging

Movement and the body

Movement is not an aura. It is not a glow round the body like the haloes that appear on television around the lucky consumers of certain breakfast cereals. Rather, movement is what the body does. It is a behavioural, bone-and-muscle affair, with nothing mystical or nebulous about it. In the Valley of Dry Bones, the recipe that brought

an army to its feet was bone, sinew, muscle, and of course the breath of life. We are starting with life as a given ingredient, and are concerned with movement as a motor matter. There is no question of some abstract quality that somehow infects the air, or puts out a rosy glow. The essence of movement is matter – body matter – and the more we can be precise about the parts of the body that we are observing, the more useful data on movement we shall collect.

When the body is in motion, one action must lead to another, and this action-sequence may be confined to the part of the body where the action originated, or spread to take in other parts as well.

You can easily observe this distinction in your own movement. Suppose you go to a public enquiry, where you want to put your views on some issue that is important to you. You must first attract attention, and to do this you raise your hand and arm, but without moving the rest of your body. This is a gesture, and as it turns out, a futile gesture, because you are not noticed. Determined not to be overlooked, you apply more energy to the movement, so that the process of actions leads on to involve your head and shoulder as well. The lift of your arm now follows through to a lift of your head, as you indicate with increasing emphasis, your wish to be heard. Now, providing the rest of your body does not move, this is still a gesture – and it is still ignored. You are now on your feet, and the arm-shoulder-head movement leads on to an upward stretch of your whole body, as you bid for

attention. This movement forces you to press your feet firmly into the floor to compensate for the shift in weight, and it goes beyond gesture. It started out as gesture, and merges into posture. It also brings the desired result – at last! The Chairman has seen you, and indicates that your point will be taken in a moment. The upward lift of your body now leads back to the slight wave of your hand with which you acknowledge the arrangement. This is posture merging into gesture.

When we observe movements of this sort, we instinctively associate the posture and gesture parts of the process, because there is a continuity and consistency of movement throughout all the involved parts of the body. Hand, arm, shoulder, head, and the rest of the body are one instrument in the total expression. But this is not necessarily so, even when most of the body is in motion, because the different parts of the body may be involved in separate action-sequences. In movement terms, you can slice yourself up, disconnecting one part of the body from another. Guests at a formal dinner can develop considerable skill in maintaining civilized behaviour above board, while kicks, squeezes and foot waggling give the lie to it down below. At home too, the mother, that domestic equivalent of the one-man-band, gives a good exhibition of disconnected action. A hand pats the dog, the other

spoons goo to the baby; a foot kicks the door shut, the other hooks the cat out of the way; head meanwhile nodding at the postman, even as the shoulder shrugs off the sort of homework question that would be best answered after a lifetime spent in the British Museum. This sort of real-life bits and pieces make child's play of games like 'flounders' or 'tops and tails', and provides the same comic element for the observer.

Many games and much amusement are based on this ability of the body to perform disconnected movements. At parties, guests are asked to twirl a tray on a finger, while wriggling a foot into a slipper, while drinking a glass of water, or some other impossible combination of actions occasionally competently carried out on the stage. All these are disconnected movements, where the action of a particular part of the body is confined to that part alone. Such incongruence of bodily action is not perceived as normal beyond a certain point, but impresses the observer with its comedy or its oddity, or strikes him as a feat of endurance. One or two disconnected gestures together may seem quite normal, but whereas you will not be surprised if a neighbour kicks a football to his son, while giving you a wave, you will feel that there is something very odd about the Hindu deity of pantomime, whose many arms act separately, in a way guaranteed to cure anyone of sighing for another pair of hands. All that unrelated activity, and a pair still left idle for mischief, soon has us wondering what is in, and what out of, hand, and glad that it really is too odd to come true!

Here the incongruity of disconnected gesture is exaggerated by a stage trick, and no unwise wishes have been granted, but some very odd effects really are produced from time to time in school gyms when pupils are set to move their arms in three time while their legs work away in four. This is the gymnastic equivalent of beating triplets against quavers, and sets the body waltzing up top, while thumping out a quickstep below, with doubtful educational results. Perhaps the achievement of this degree of bodily control has a certain fascination and challenge, because disconnected gestures also figure in some of the complicated skipping and clapping games that children play.

Whatever the motives for these performances they all require fierce concentration to achieve the degree of control proportionate to the number of disconnected gestures involved, and they are characterized by a lack of flow between the parts of the body, so that the more exaggerated the gestures, the more striking the disharmony.

Disconnected gesture probably reaches its ultimate exaggeration in the one-man-band, where the whole body is in motion, but all the parts perform separate actions, the foot controls the drum, the knee

clashes the cymbals, the fingers pluck strings, the head jingles the bells and the lips tootle the flute. These various gesture processes can only be maintained by extreme conscious control, and it is this deliberate forcing of bodily behaviour from its normal pattern that arouses both our uneasy admiration, and our sense of relief when the whirligig comes to a halt. The peformance makes us feel uncomfortable, whereas if we were watching the fluid movements of yoga exercises, we would feel soothed, and of course this discomfort is also shared by the performer. If you watch the bandsman closely, you will notice that he takes advantage of a momentary pause to fit in a posture movement, among the whirl of disconnected gestures, and if you try to imitate his expertise, you will find that this adjustment comes as a great relief – in fact an essential relief. As you quickly discover for yourself, no one can last out for long as a performer of disconnected gestures, without introducing a posture movement. Experiments show that the average lengths of endurance is only three minutes before there must be a posture movement that renews the sense of co-operation between the parts of the body. The nature of movement is apparently co-operative, so that actions which take no account of the whole body are both felt and seen to be a source of discomfort, and cannot be maintained for any length of time. Even the highly skilled bandsman, who must slip a postural adjustment into his performance as best he may, cannot manage without it.

Most of us earn our livings in less physically exacting ways than the one-man-band, and we can and do continually integrate, or merge our posture and gesture movements throughout our everyday life. This process of posture–gesture merging, or PGM, is the norm of movement behaviour. It is this process, whereby actions are not performed independently but flow into each other, which is at the root of the movement behaviour of modern man, and it is to PGM that we must look for the interpretation of non-verbal behaviour. PGM is the key to the secret language of movement.

Posture–gesture merging in detail

Although we can unlock the secrets of the body and interpret the speaking silence of movement with the PGM key, we must look closely at its nature before using it. Finding keys and unlocking doors can be quite different matters. Alice in Wonderland, you will recall, found the golden key to the garden door, but through some trifling mismanagements and curious mishaps went for a swim in her pool of tears, instead of a stroll in the garden. If our key is to be of use it must be properly handled, and fitted to the right lock! We have a good start by establishing that the essential quality of PGM is flow of movement. Perhaps we can find out more if we examine this merging process in detail, continuing where we left off at the imaginary public enquiry, where we first saw it in action.

You will remember that, at the imaginary public enquiry, it became apparent that the body could be used as a single harmonious instrument for self-expression. At the outset of your attempt to secure the Chairman's attention, you raised your arm without moving the rest of your body. This was a gesture which, as your excitement or determination got the better of you, you expanded to include a head and shoulder movement, finally rising to your feet, causing your gesture to merge into posture as your whole body became involved in an expression of urgency. Gesture became merged into posture, so that the movement exhibited PGM, but the merging was only possible because the quality of movement was consistent throughout, and there

was no interruption of flow. If there had been an inconsistency or break in the movement, there would have been no merging.

To illustrate this, we must alter our scenario a little. We now imagine that the paper you were using to signal to the Chairman slipped from your fingers. If you were momentarily irritated by this, you might have gritted your teeth, or clicked your tongue. Obviously both these actions are mere gestures, so there would be no question of posture–gesture merging. If you had tried to retrieve matters by grabbing the paper as it slipped, but rather awkwardly, since you could not afford to remove your attention from the platform, then your back might have hollowed in a convex movement, although the normal grabbing movement would be a concave one. This contradiction would prevent any posture movement from occurring, since posture, by definition involves the whole body in consistent expression. Once again, there is no question of merging, since there is no posture movement.

However, if there had been both posture and gesture, merging might still not occur. If you had raised your arm in gesture, paused

momentarily, and then grabbed as the paper slipped from your fingers, this time using a consistent concave postural movement, there would none the less be no merging – no PGM. This is because your posture–gesture movement in detail was: slow gesture – pause – quick posture.

Not only was there inconsistency in the quality of movement between the gesture and the posture – from slow to quick – but also an interruption of flow due to the pause. On the other hand, if your grab, or teeth-gritting, or tongue-clicking were followed through by a consistent postural movement without pause or inconsistency between the gesture and the posture, then PGM would be exhibited in the movement. Your whole body would have been involved either in catching the paper, or, perhaps, in a braced posture of protest of the 'This is the last straw' variety. Either way, your whole body would have passed from the original gesture into the total expression of posture without pause or inconsistency, and there would have been a genuine merging of gesture into posture. So far as PGM is concerned consistency is a jewel, and he who hesitates is lost!

The same considerations hold true when PGM occurs as posture merges back into gesture. At the enquiry, your urgent posture attracted the Chairman's notice, and passed to gesture, as you acknowledge with a nod or a wave. If this gesture had followed the

posture movement without a break in the continuity, and, being merely a quietened-down version of the movement, had been carried out without change in the quality, merging would have occurred. If, however you had burst into derisory laughter as the Chairman looked your way, stopping in embarrassment under his glare, and finally clapping your hand to your mouth to stifle the eruption, the pause would segregate the posture and gesture in your movement, and the break in continuity would almost certainly cause the quality of the gesture to differ from that of the original posture. Of course it is perfectly possible to burst into laughter *with* PGM. If you had exploded with mirth, and then clapped your hand to your mouth as you quietened down this would almost certainly be a gesture arising from the posture without break or inconsistency, since it merely extends the ebbing of your laughter.

As you can see, we can now take another step forward and assert with confidence, as a result of our investigations, that the presence of PGM depends on the absence of segregation in posture movement – or more simply: no segregation with PGM.

Merging and segregation: spontaneity and contrivance

In movement, postures and gestures must either be merged or remain segregated, and, in any given period, the proportion of PGM to segregation in the total movement can vary from nothing to 100 per cent.

If by way of experiment, you try to prevent any merging for a ten-minute period, either of gesture into posture or vice versa, you will soon be tired and irritable. The process is difficult and uncomfortable, and requires a great deal of self-control. What is more, your behaviour will seem stilted and put-on to others, and everyone will be aware of its lack of spontaneity and naturalness. Here is a quick and effective way of convincing yourself that segregation in posture–gesture movement precludes spontaneity, and has to be contrived with effort. Conversely, contrived or put-on behaviour necessitates the segregation of posture and gesture, which also requires effort.

This correlation of effort and contrivance with segregation in movement is supported by findings from a series of interview-observations. Where the level of movement-segregation was observed to be unusually high, the people interviewed proved, on further investigation, to have set out to create a false impression. They were for a variety of reasons, and for the duration of the interviews, amateur 'con' men. If they had been professional confidence tricksters, the observers' skills

would have been even more severely tested, for the true 'con' man brings considerable expertise to the practice of contrived behaviour, which not only accustoms him to segregating his posture and gesture, but also to segregating it in ways that are not obvious. His 'con' is put across in a capable, plausible manner, designed to minimize the sense of unease, which your own experiment has shown to be the usual result of such behaviour.

When you become aware of a high degree of posture–gesture segregation at any meeting or interview, you may or may not be up against the Mafia or tête-à-tête with the underworld, but you can be sure that something is awry. For some reason, the people you are with do not feel free to behave naturally. They may be embarrassed, or annoyed, or nervous, or feel that they are in a false position, or an unsympathetic environment. Your immediate reaction will almost certainly be to wish that so-and-so would just 'be himself', and this hits the nail on the head, because the root cause of our uneasiness is his not being himself. Although the immediate cause of discomfort, is all those uncomfortable segregated movements, the source of these is the necessity, real or imagined, to conceal the real self. Attempts to make someone feel at home spring as much from the desire to eliminate this uneasiness, as from kindliness. Your guest is assumed to 'be himself' at home, and so, if you can create a home from home for him, those discomforting segregated movements should begin to merge into soothing PGM. We want him to 'consider himself part of the furniture' as the song has it, so that we can consider him as little as part of the furniture!

You can check up on this by examining what happens at the other extreme of the spontaneity–contrivance scale, when behaviour is at its most natural. Keep an eye on a friend when he seems at his best or in good form, and you will be sure to find that his postures and gestures merge in and out of each other, and that there is little segregation. Suppose your friend is deep in conversation with someone he likes and trusts, so that the talk is free and easy, and both parties are spontaneous and natural. At such a meeting there will be a plethora of

gestures used, even though the English are usually more sparing of these than other nationalities. There will be many gestures of the hand and arm, along with shrugs, nods, and facial movements. You will notice too that the inevitable posture movements with which they are interspersed will be very fully merged with them. It will strike you that your friend is 'being himself' with an easy spontaneity, and normally you would be attracted to introduce yourself, and join in.

Unfortunately, you have taken it on yourself to play the investigator, and if you decide that it is justifiable to spoil the fun in the interests of your researches, you have only to hover nearby with a notebook and pencil, regretting that you cannot join the party, but would be very glad if the pair of them could just carry on quite naturally. You can only want to jot down a few notes on their behaviour! This may do irreparable damage to your friendship, but it is guaranteed to further your investigation into body language. Watch how self-consciousness ruins the spontaneity of the get-together!

Gradually your friend's posture and gesture movements cease to merge, and become segregated into stiff, isolated actions, as his behaviour grows stilted under your gimlet eye. Unless your friend is a practised 'con' man, you will become aware, if you know him well enough, that he is not being himself, not behaving naturally. Even if he is a good and determined actor, this will still happen, since he cannot produce PGM to order. At best, he could only hope to deceive you by a practised performance of segregated gestures, not usually within the capacity of anyone other than a habitual deceiver.

If you flinch from so drastic an experiment, and value your friend-ships, perhaps it would be wiser to be your own guinea-pig. This time you must induce self-consciousness in yourself. This is not in the least difficult. You have only to start to watch your own behaviour with conscious consideration, and sure enough your posture and gesture sequences will separate out like cream from milk. As you look in the mirror to smile at yourself, you will realize that the smile looks put on, because this smile is confined to gesture only, whereas, if you were genuinely amused your smiling gesture would merge into an amused posture. The mirror-smile reminds you of a doll or puppet, and explains why someone too tired to be amused, but forced to act sociably, will complain of smiling 'until I thought my face would crack'. Smiles of genuine amusement look and feel natural.

The difference between contrived and spontaneous behaviour, and its significance, is often missed entirely by the 'best' photographers. In fact the better their reputation *as* photographers, the more likely they are to be absorbed in the technicalities, and fail to produce portraits that give satisfaction. 'Head a leetle more to the right, please' – 'eyes a leetle more to the right' – 'ah, *quite* still, please', Click! Another portrait with every muscle correctly positioned, and every tooth perfectly lit. How unreasonable of the sitter to object; 'it doesn't look a bit like me!' It is however a perfectly valid objection, since the photographer has entirely prevented a natural merging of posture and gesture, by setting the body rigidly, and adding a smiling gesture as an extra. No wonder the smile looks forced. An amateur photographer would not stand a chance of getting away with this sort of thing.

Every sunny corner of a thousand holiday resorts echoes to the protests of snapshot victims. 'Get *on* with it! Tell us when to smile for pity's sake. We can't keep saying 'Cheese' while you take a camera course, my poor face feels quite stiff!' and the like. Everyone feels instinctively that a natural photo depends on slick timing to prevent spontaneity fading into self-consciousness, although no one would be likely to ascribe this death of spontaneity to the onset of segregated movements and the disappearance of PGM. Professional observations of movement show that these feelings have a sound basis, even if their rationale is not appreciated. Observers, rating people's behaviour for its sincerity and naturalness, have found that the higher the score, the greater the PGM in the movement. There is, in fact, a correlation not only between segregation and contrivance, but also between merging and spontaneity, when movement is translated into behaviour.

PGM and movement skills

Whereas a confidence man must aim at performing segregated movements in a plausible manner, so that his victim's unease is not aroused, the task is reversed when we want to learn a new movement skill. This time we must achieve merging, because we are aiming at an easy flow of movement, produced with economy of effort. Now, since posture–gesture merging does not occur unless the quality of movement is the same in both posture and gesture, and since hesitations and pauses must be removed, it is hardly surprising that we feel hopelessly awkward and clumsy when we set out to acquire a new skill. Worse still, others who already have this skill, even if they are ready to be as helpful as possible, are inclined to wonder secretly what can be the matter with us. They have not really got the faintest inkling of our problem, and would be amazed to hear that we are suffering from a lack of PGM. We simply cannot make the postural adjustments that are appropriate to the necessary gestures, although we may master these easily enough. Since we cannot achieve the even flow of movement, which is essential for PGM, spontaneity and naturalness elude us. It is this failure to achieve PGM that results in exhaustion and clumsiness.

You can observe this, in an extreme form, at village fetes or church bazaars, where various competitions have been devised which not only demand a new skill, but also make its acquisition difficult or impossible. Why do we find it so difficult to move a ring along a bended wire without touching the one on the other? It is because we need to make a postural adjustment as our hand moves the ring along the wire, but, if we do make this movement, the ring touches the wire and sets off the bell. Ping! Next please! Similarly, drawing shapes in a mirror, prevents us making the adjustments that would bring success, by hopelessly confusing us. However, we are always convinced beforehand that we shall achieve a spontaneity and natural ease which will carry off the prize, because we never spot the trick by which these are precluded, and a PGM performance denied us.

The quality of naturalness or spontaneity in movement is what distinguishes the skilled performer from the tyro. Movement skills are, perhaps, most strikingly exhibited at the circus, or in the gym, because here the movement itself is the central attraction, whereas in sport, or ballet or ice-shows, the movement is subordinated to some other end, such as winning, or linked to some other ingredient, such as a fairy-tale, or music. At the circus or in the gym, however, movement skill is often demonstrated for its own sake, and perhaps as we watch such a demonstration, the first thing that strikes us is how easy it all looks. The juggler's paraphernalia is weightless and apparently exempt from the laws of gravity, while the tightrope walker clearly has hooks on his feet, and the bareback rider glue on his shoes. Perfectly relaxed, the performers fly across the big top, or float from mount to mount, or levitate into aerial somersaults. Indeed, it is all made to look so easy that the performance is in danger of defeating its object, and the audience must be reminded of its skill. The trapeze artist introduces a wobble, or clowns rush into the ring and take off performers, imitating their feats on tightrope or horseback, but with some new ingredient that suddenly makes the show look, in spite of the evidence of our eyes, not merely difficult but downright impossible!

If you watch such a performance carefully, contrasting the ease of

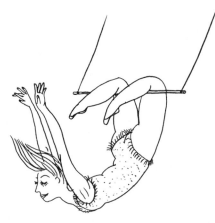

the artists with the clumsiness of the clowns, you will realize that the easiness comes from complete mastery of PGM in any action. The artists have eliminated from their movements any disharmony of quality or suggestion of interruption. The mocking clowns on the other hand, introduce disconnected postures and gestures into the same actions, so that unevenness of quality and awkward interruption destroy the flow of the movement, and produce an appearance of clumsiness and effort. Of course in the circus, the clown is putting on an act. He is pretending the absence of PGM, and the skill of his performance is really very great. If PGM were as absent as he makes out, he would undoubtedly fall off the horse or tightrope in ways that would be hurtful and distressing instead of amusing, exactly as we would ourselves if we attempted circus feats with the lack of PGM and the disconnected movements pretended by the clown. His clowning highlights the nature of our difficulties in learning new skills. We quite genuinely cannot make the postural adjustments appropriate to the gestures we require. If we want to see this difficulty caricatured outside the circus, we have only to watch Tommy Cooper on television!

Since the mastery of a new skill depends on the achievement of PGM, you might think that coaches, trainers and teachers would concentrate their efforts on this problem. But in fact this rarely happens! The teacher starts, as he must, with the required gesture, showing the student how to grip and turn the spanner, how to hold and swing a racquet, or how to flip the pancake with a jerk of the frying-pan. Usually he will realize that this is not enough, and go on to suggest an appropriate posture of the 'stand straight, left leg forward, shoulders back' variety. This is just the sort of instruction which a photographer might give his sitter, but whereas the photographer wants stillness, the teacher of movement skills wants the right series of movements. Stance alone is only a starting-point. We are not statues, and it is the process of postural adjustment to the required gestures that we need to learn. However, if the teacher is not a movement specialist, the real movement skill will be left out of the training altogether, and may or may not be supplied haphazardly by the student himself.

You can observe this failure to appreciate the importance of postural adjustment on any beach where people are playing ball games with very young children. The child is placed at arm's length, and his arms lifted into position to catch the ball. Then it is lobbed gently into place. 'Well done. Try again!' This time the ball reaches the child a mere fraction higher in the air, or a mite to left or right. All the same, it bumps him on the nose, or flops past him. Why? Because that slight

step back, or bend, to one side, that minute postural adjustment has not taken place. He was told to stand just so, and he has, and now everyone shouts, 'don't just stand there!' Probably no one notices any deficiency in the instruction, and after a few more cries of 'Butter-fingers', the adjustments will be made without any help. The child has not been taught the movement skill; he has discovered it for himself.

It is this teach-yourself ability that a teacher instinctively assesses in a pupil. A driving instructor can often tell by the way a learner opens the car door, settles into the seat, and grasps the wheel, whether he is fifteen lessons from his test or fifty. A craft teacher will flinch as a child picks up the scissors to cut out a soft toy, struck by a foreboding that blood and sweat will not produce so much as a felt mouse by open day, and a piano teacher will go down on her knees to parents to beg them to find some other road to fame for their prodigy. Although the best teachers will succeed in drawing out any aptitude that exists, and the worst must rely on self-teaching pupils, a lot of time and effort could be saved all round if students were directed towards rewarding activities. This is more likely when the basis of movement skills is properly

understood. Aptitude, which the teacher instinctively sizes up, depends on the degree to which the essential qualities of movement required for an activity match the innate quality of the student's PGM. If there is close correlation, there is real aptitude; if not, the teacher must expect difficulties, especially if he has no idea how to compensate for the missing quality in the PGM, and is impatient or intolerant of its absence.

Most of us, setting out to acquire a skill, sense our innate aptitude for ourselves, judging it from what is happening in our movement. If we 'see' just how to do it, or get the 'feel' or 'hang' of it easily, then we have achieved a good measure of PGM at an early stage, because the required movements suit well with our PGM, whereas if we are all fingers and thumbs, choosing a left-handed way of going on, and despairing of ever learning the technique, then the quality of movement required is probably badly at variance with our innate PGM. If so, we must either take exceptional time and trouble to acquire this particular skill, or settle for another. The good news is that there has to be something else more suitable. We all inescapably move with PGM, and so inevitably have our own PGM characteristics which are suitable for certain skills. These may not be the skills that are well-rewarded, or in short supply, or highly approved, but it does mean that out PGM is as good as anyone else's if it is applied in the right area – right, that is, for us.

Once you accept that your sort of PGM has its own particular qualities, that you have what we shall call a PGM pattern, and that others have PGM patterns that are radically different to our own, you can more easily understand the wide variety of aptitudes that people display, and become more tolerant all round of failure and more hopeful of success, when you try to master the skills best suited to you. It will be apparent that one person may not be able to climb a staircase, let alone a mountain, without falling over his own feet, but may be full of PGM when sweeping around a stage, obtaining a sympathetic

response from an audience. The precise movements that make a good dentist or musician may escape you, but the wide-ranging movements that make a good compere, or a comedian, or manager may come easily to you.

It is this individuality in movement styles or PGM patterns that leads to type-casting. It is appreciated that certain movements come naturally to – that is, are performed with PGM by – certain people, and so they are cast in parts that emphasize this sort of action. They may be habitually cast as the sort of people who fill the stage or set with wide-ranging atmospheric qualities such as witches or panto dames, and not cast as characters with definite blocking qualities such as giants, policemen and royalty. This happens most to individuals in whom one particular quality seems especially predominant. John Wayne, for example, is the block-type *par excellence*. He is like a great block of granite on the set, where there is no getting past him, and no getting anything out of him. His favourite entrance is head on into the middle of the set, and his typical exit is a measured retreat bisecting middle-distance. Theatre wings would be a disaster for him! Clearly these sort of blocking movements are the ones that come naturally to him, or correspond with his PGM. Charlton Heston on the other hand operates in vast sweeping or enclosing movements that give you the impression that there are no boundaries anywhere in the horizontal lane, while Groucho Marx slices back and forth into the environment using his characteristic PGM pattern. We could reasonably suspect that John Wayne's undoubted screen quality would be impossible in live theatre, that Charlton Heston would not inspire confidence as a dentist, and that Groucho Marx would feel frustrated as an academic, because their PGM patterns are out of kilter with such activities.

The PGM pattern

Studies of PGM in different individuals show that in each person's movement, certain qualities are always present. For each individual, there is a distinctive PGM pattern – a sort of signature tune in movement. This remains true regardless of the type of behaviour observed. Gardening, dining, relaxing, and even asleep, an individual's PGM pattern retains its particular distinctive characteristics. Nor does it make the slightest difference how the person happens to be feeling, whether sad, happy, excited, carefree, bored, in love, or out. Even

actors who portray all these activities and emotions in quick succession
retain the same PGM pattern throughout their many roles. The
pattern is only obliterated if posture is separated from gesture, due to
some constraint on spontaneous behaviour, and even then, the trained
analyst can infer its nature by examining observation records of the
separate postures and gestures.

This PGM pattern can be analysed from any valid sample of a
person's body movement, and although a reliable sample must consist
of several hundred observations, these can be obtained within two to
three hours. Adequate data can be collected in this period to establish
the qualities of the pattern under observation, and once analysed, the
findings stand the test of time. Patterns of posture–gesture merging
remain constant throughout adult life, and analyses of the same
pattern at fifteen-year intervals show little variation in the individual
characteristics. The police, putting fingerprints on file, know that the
same prints turning up fifteen years later can safely be used for
identification, and, in the same way our PGM patterns last a lifetime,
and there is no need to take new samples as time passes. We are, as it
were, hallmarked with our patterns and, if we can understand them,
we learn something of a long-term value about ourselves.

You can see very clearly the value of the PGM key, and the
importance of learning to observe PGM patterns from one of Rudyard
Kipling's well-known *Just So Stories*. Painted Jaguar's tummy remained
empty, although his paw was filled with prickles, due to confusion of
identity between Hedgehog and Tortoise. To help him, his mother
devised what we could regard as a child's guide to posture pattern and
her young hopeful recited; to himself;

> Can't curl, but can swim –
> Slow-solid, that's him!
> Curls up, but can't swim –
> Stickly-Prickly that's him!

Hedgehog and Tortoise only escaped this disastrous analysis of
their characteristic movements, by going to the limits of effort and
contrivance to alter their behaviour, becoming, as you will remember,
the first Armadilloes. This story neatly illustrates our discovery that
spontaneous behaviour springs from movements that fall within the
PGM pattern. The more a person's movements are performed with
PGM, the more his behaviour is observed to be spontaneous,
characteristic and sincere.

As Painted Jaguar's mother pointed out, a hedgehog is a hedgehog, and a tortoise is a tortoise. If a person acts outside his PGM pattern, he is judged to be acting, not only in a contrived manner, but also uncharacteristically. Mother Jaguar's advice, on hearing that there was an animal behaving as part-Tortoise and part-Hedgehog, was to call it 'Armadillo' until a proper name could be put to it, and this is sound advice for our purposes. We all behave characteristically when our PGM patterns are in spontaneous action, and this behaviour reveals who we are.

Once we know this, we can observe spontaneity in our own behaviour to see when we are expressing ourselves fully as people, and when we are subject to constraints. When the action-sequences in your own movement or that of others begin and end as gesture only, you will ask yourself why are you forced into calculated behaviour that prevents you being other than you are, and when you find that your gestures are merging in and out of your posture movement you will assess the circumstances and company in which you find this freedom to be yourself. We are all forced into calculated behaviour by social pressures, and as a result become subject to stress, and we all form relationships in which we cannot express ourselves fully. Often we are not aware of the pressures that are making us behave uncharacteristically, and so we cannot exercise proper judgment in the choice of our circumstances or colleagues. Understanding the significance of the PGM pattern you can become more discerning of the

nature and causes of your own behaviour – and that of others.

You can test the reliability of the link between PGM movement and characteristic behaviour by a simple experiment. Select a habit which is performed as a disconnected gesture. Perhaps one of you drums on the table, and the other rubs the side of his nose? Now try to do away with these habits. If no PGM is involved and the action is confined to gesture, then you will succeed, but if it is performed with PGM, as is usual with nail-biting or thumb-sucking, then it will be very difficult to eradicate, as any mother will know. Indeed, since the habit is a characteristic expression of the personality, the necessary constraint and effort required to remove it may be misplaced.

Here then is the PGM key to the self, the means of self-expression by which identity is revealed in movement. With it we can unlock the secret silence of non-verbal behaviour. We have found it by a careful examination of what the body does in movement, bringing something vital and valuable from our Valley of Dry Bones by:

1 Establishing that gestures and postural adjustments involve a sequence of movement, not a single action.

2 Observing that one action changes to another when there is a change in one or more of the movement-components – timing, direction, and pressure – causing a break in the flow or quality of movement.

3 Examining action-sequences to distinguish those confined to gesture, and those merged with posture.

4 Correlating PGM movements and spontaneity or sincerity.

5 Concluding that PGM movement expresses the self, and does so through a distinctive pattern.

We have also tested our PGM key, finding it useful and reliable. We can now discover what secrets it will unlock.

7
The PGM key: self-expression and motivation

A key will unlock the door for which it is designed. Its value to you will depend on your own motivation. If you are half-frozen you will prefer to have the key to the coal-hole rather than the key to the cellar, unless you share the convictions of the coachman who poured brandy in his boots to warm his feet. On the other hand, if you have a good fire but feel a trifle chilly, the key to a well-stocked cellar might provide a preferable inner warmth, provided that you put your brandy in the conventional place. Your preference however makes not one iota of difference; no amount of wishing will fit the coal-hole key to the cellar door or vice versa.

The PGM key also unlocks one particular door, leaving others closed. If you have carried out the checks and experiments in the last chapter, you will probably agree that the PGM pattern is a genuine mode of self-expression, which can be discerned by perceptive observers behind the gesture front that is adopted to screen the personality. It expresses the personality as it really is, whereas the front exists when expression is mainly through segregated postures and gestures. The PGM pattern expresses the 'real you'. Everyone must have a PGM pattern, and these patterns differ from one another, each one being unique. The PGM key is, then, designed to unlock the self.

There are, however, a variety of doors to the self, and the most obvious one is not the one that is designed to fit! It does not allow us to discriminate between the qualities of different PGM patterns. We cannot assess the richness and value of individual patterns of expression, rating some better and some worse than others and awarding points as is usual, for example, in testing for intelligence. PGM patterns can probably be judged more or less valuable for certain limited purposes, and better or worse in certain specific circumstances, but generally speaking no qualitative judgment is valid, and we are not enabled to use the PGM key as a means of discriminating between individuals. Any such judgments would depend on many other considerations such as culture, vocation, class and so on, all of which would affect our opinions as to what constituted richness or value in PGM expression. It is wiser to accept that my PGM pattern is right for me, and yours for you, which is exactly what we do when we refuse to be forced to act outside of our patterns in ways that do not feel right. 'I'll do it my way', we say, 'yours may be OK for you, but it's just not *me*!' Instinctively, we select methods of operation in line with our individual self-expression, and avoid those which are alien, and do not allow us to be ourselves. No one, except by contrivance, can act as other than himself, and the PGM pattern is the distillation of each person's distinctive and individual mode of expression. It is these secrets of self-expression which the PGM key is designed to unlock, and we can hope to find out, as we turn the key in this door, both the sort of self-expression that is manifested through the PGM pattern, and what it can tell us about the individual personality.

The PGM mode of self-expression

The mode of expression through PGM is different from what is expressed in speech and far more significant. The limitations of speech in communication between people are obvious. A law court has procedures especially developed to ensure that the spoken word shall give a true picture of events, and yet anyone who has sat on a jury will know that its members interpret the words or even the most expert summing up by the most explicit of judges differently, and that they are influenced by non-verbal communication from the accused, the witness and the counsel, regardless of the words spoken. An eminent barrister predicted recently that, in ten years' time, judges will be directing the attention of the jury to the postures and gestures of the accused or of witnesses rather than the spoken evidence, 'The jury may consider', the judge may well say, 'that the arm and head gestures accompanying the accused's protestations of innocence denote insincerity – but you may read them as an expression of genuine conviction. It is for you to decide'. Juries, like the rest of us, try to establish sincerity as much by the language of movement as by words. Words not only suffer from the limitations imposed by language and interpretation, but may or may not be sincere. If words are used, whether in court or elsewhere, that are out of accord with the PGM pattern of the speaker, then we instinctively feel that he is insincere. This means that we recognize the PGM pattern as a more valid mode

of expression than speech, and this conclusion is supported by a variety of experiments. For instance, the sincerity or otherwise of the host's welcome to each of a stream of guests was assessed by observers from the evidence of PGM. Various hosts were studied, and notes compared with them afterwards showed that the true feelings of the speakers had been assessed with remarkable accuracy from their movements, and that the speech is a more deceitful mode of expression than movement. The speech of the speaking silence is far more basic than verbal speech. You cannot deceive through PGM expression.

The PGM pattern is also a mode of expression of a different order to its components, posture and gesture. Languages of gestures are usually culturally specialized, and do not tell us anything about the individual personality. They have the character of deaf and dumb language, while a style of posture, such as a militaristic bearing, reveals nothing vital about the individual other than the degree to which he succeeds or fails to meet the established postural norm. The PGM pattern, on the other hand, expresses some sort of core of individual behaviour, so that the individual acts out in his PGM the distinctiveness of his own personality, saying in movement, 'This is me'.

In spite of the obvious potential of body movement for the detective story, these usually rely much more heavily on the components of PGM than on the PGM pattern for identification of the criminal. This is because few who-dunnits are concerned with the underlying motivation for the crime or the personality of the murderer. The plot turns on the skill and methods employed to discover him, a routine motive being supplied without any real attempt to relate it to the personality concerned. Dr Joseph Bell, the original for Sherlock Holmes, told his guests that a good detective should be able to tell a stranger's occupation, habits, past history and nationality immediately. Although he listed gait and mannerisms, the Holmes deductions rely much more heavily on such items as callouses, tattoo marks, scars, gestural habits, clothing peculiarities and marks, and general appearance. Movement is very little exploited, because in Conan Doyle's day the causes of behaviour were not as sought after as they are now. Although the PGM pattern is as distinctive as fingerprints, and a good detective should be able to distinguish an individual by it, as he might recognize his face from a police identikit, and although its characteristics are not only unique, but cannot be removed by plastic surgery, the recognition of the individual from his pattern of movement and the attempt to read the meaning of this movement is still little exploited either in books or in everyday life.

Much preliminary work has, however, already been done on both sides of the Atlantic to establish its significance. Over the years, we have undertaken the study of over eight thousand people, analysing their PGM patterns from reliable samples of their posture–gesture movement. As we have found already, the PGM pattern is usually present in its totality in any two-to-three-hour period of waking activity, and observations taken over this length of time are usually adequate for analysis. Some two hundred persons have been re-studied at intervals of up to eighteen years, and more than three thousand have been followed up in some degree, some continuously, over twenty years. The subjects have been mainly British, but have included many Americans and Europeans and a more limited number of Africans and Asians.

These investigations have led us to a number of conclusions about the nature of the PGM pattern.

1 There is no limit to the different ways in which the PGM pattern can express individual behaviour.

2 No two PGM patterns are the same, although groupings may be made by type, and the link with national characteristics, psychological typing and other measurements of personality traits is open to investigation.

3 Individual PGM patterns remain the same from physical maturity until death with only marginal variance, unless the individual suffers some highly abnormal or traumatic experience, such as ruthless brainwashing or major therapy.

4 Marginal changes in the PGM pattern can be significant for personal development.

5 PGM pattern is probably inherited, since most of its constituents can be detected during childhood.

It would appear, then, that the PGM pattern has the utmost significance as a mode of expression for the personality, and that it can give essential information about the individual. This is the door through which the PGM key allows us to reach the self.

The door to personal motivation

Assuming accuracy in our analysis of the PGM pattern, we can now see to what sort of information about ourselves this mode of self-expression can lead us. Are we to be let in to the coal-hole or to the cellar? Certainly this door does not lead to the airy attics of the intelligence. It seems unlikely that the PGM pattern can contribute to the measurement of intelligence, although some recent researchers have thought otherwise, and it does not lead to the workshop, in that it does not measure skill, nor does it lead to secret places of divination, since it does not allow predictions of specific acts of performance. However, the foundations of personality *are* unlocked by the PGM pattern and it hardly matters whether we think of them as cellar or coal-hole or subterranean passage, because the pattern reveals the long-term motivation of the individual and on this foundation his behaviour is firmly based.

The discovery of individual motivation through the PGM pattern is as rich in its implications as that of Ali Baba, and the possession of the riches is equally dependent on the correct password. An understanding of motivations is, for instance, far more valuable than assessments of intelligence or the prediction of someone's future actions, because its roots go deeper into the personality. No assessment of intelligence can tell you to what use that intelligence may be put, no rating of skills tells you where they should be applied, and the prediction of actions has the hit-and-miss quality of fortune-telling, or the ambivalence of the Delphic circle. An understanding of individual motivation, the driving force that decides behaviour, gives a basis for prediction of a quite different order. From accurate analysis of the PGM pattern, you can tell not only how an individual will choose to behave whenever circumstances permit his freedom of choice, but also indicate the circumstances which he should choose for himself wherever possible in order to make the most creative use of his individual characteristics.

The open sesame to this behavioural treasure is our understanding of the compelling force of the PGM pattern as a motive for behaviour. We have already investigated the way in which PGM pattern is always present in a sample of behaviour, and can even be deduced from fragmented behaviour when the pattern is not being consistently applied. It is clear that the pattern represents some 'core' of individual behaviour, so that when it is applied, the individual acts out his distinctive personality in his unique pattern of movement, saying silently 'this is me'. It is, however, his compulsion to act in this way that is of vital importance. An individual must reveal himself in this manner. Whenever circumstances allow, he will express his personality through his PGM pattern. So great is this power and pull of the pattern as a motivation to action, that no one can successfully resist, withhold, or conceal it. The PGM pattern is always there, always struggling, as it were, to get out. If it is constrained in one direction, it will escape in another; if it is forced to hide, it will find a thousand secret ways for its expression.

Writing his classic *Thirty-Nine Steps* some thirty years after Conan Doyle invented Holmes, John Buchan made his plot turn on characteristic movement. The villain was revealed by his manner of tapping his fingers on his knees, not that is, because he performed this action, but because he performed it in a particular way.

It was movement I remembered . . . a little thing lasting only a second, and the odds were a thousand to one that I might have . . . missed it. But I didn't, and in a flash . . . I was looking . . . with full and absolute recognition.

Whereas in *The Blue Carbuncle* Holmes had astounded Watson by deducing occupation, fate and alcoholism from a hat, Buchan had grasped at the secrets of non-verbal behaviour, which he cites as far more basic.

Peter once discussed with me the question of disguises, and he had a theory which struck me . . . He said, barring absolute certainties like fingerprints, mere physical traits were very little use for identification . . . The only thing that mattered was what Peter called 'atmosphere'. . . . If a man could get into perfectly different surroundings, from those in which he had first been observed, and – this is the important part – really play up to these surroundings and behave as though he had never been out of them, he would puzzle the cleverest detectives on earth.

The emphasis on behaviour is Buchan's. He had already appreciated the importance of PGM for identification and the necessity of concealing it to escape detection, and he also recognized that PGM will escape somewhere even if constrained, by arranging a denouncement based on a tiny characteristic movement.

The constraint necessary for a fugitive may be of an unusual degree, since the self must be entirely concealed, but in everyday life PGM expression is frequently frustrated. The causes of such frustration range from such gross physical necessities as extreme thirst or hunger to less serious social constraints. At the extreme, physical need will exert so great a motivational force as to exclude other motivation, while the less serious constraints prevent an individual from applying his PGM pattern to the full, and arise from unsuitable work, material tension, financial problems, family stress, social insecurity, ill-health, or indeed any other circumstances creating a sense of failure and stress, especially those involving too-rapid change and over-heavy responsibilities. All or any of these, constrain us to behave in ways that cramp and falsify our self-expression.

Since no one can hope to escape all constraint in everyday living, the effects of the denial of the PGM pattern are experienced by everyone. We are all at times frustrated, constrained, over-burdened and harried, and forced, as a result, at work or in personal relationships, or even at leisure, to act through an increased proportion of segregated gesture, and a decreased allowance of PGM. The greater the proportion of segregation to PGM, the worse we feel. Even though the activity carried out in this way may be, if measured objectively, entirely effective and successful, it has to be paid for in ways that range from headaches and irritability to serious breakdown and personality disorders. To say that a person must express himself is by no means as obvious as it sounds; the pressures and temptations to role-playing in-

clude matters as important to most of us as job success, social acceptance, family and sexual status. None the less, if you engineer yourself
or others a denial of personality, you are conniving at, or are the victim
of, real self-destruction of the type condemned in the New Testa-
ment, when Christ pointed out that to call a person a fool is tant-
amount to murder. It is the man who is fully and at all times himself
who has attained the ultimate creative freedom.

Fortunately, the circumstances which would lead to total repression
would be so extreme as to be very unusual. The usual effect of the
degree of a constraint we experience is minor physical distress, and a
reduction of creativity in our behaviour. It is apparent, however, that
in those areas of our living where we can choose our circumstances, the
most constructive choices are those which free our personalities and
allow as full expression as possible in the free flow of our particular

PGM pattern. This is by no means a licence to do as we like, but on the contrary to found our decisions in education, career selection, choice of marriage partner and companions, and leisure-time pursuits in a disciplined way, on sound criteria. The importance of this for health, happiness, and ultimate personal fulfilment is immense. It is also normally within everyone's reach. If you find that you are under constraint at work, it becomes that much more essential for you to achieve release through your leisure, and conversely, if you cannot be yourself at home, then your choice of job or friends becomes much more critical. Since the expression of the self through PGM depends less on the what is done than on the way it is done, quite small alterations in circumstances or approach can often have far-reaching effects. There is also available for everyone the safety-valve of ritual. So powerful in its motivational drive is the PGM pattern that it produces for its expression a form of ritualistic behaviour not found at all stages of man's development, but predominantly characteristic of modern industrialized man.

Ritual and the significance of PGM

The PGM pattern decides what movement will constantly recur in a person's day-to-day behaviour; it is a collection of those bits of movement that are always present in a sample of his movement behaviour. This is by no means all the movement he makes, but other movement is transient and temporary in character, may be eradicated by training, may change or be discarded, and is used in passing as technique, game or socially contrived device. It has no real personal significance. The PGM pattern, on the other hand, has a vital importance to him, and is retained for life with only marginal modification, except in the exceptional circumstances of personality breakdown. There is a compulsion to act within the PGM pattern of a beneficial, rather than a neurotic, character. Acting out our PGM patterns makes us feel good, and brings personal satisfaction.

The compulsive nature of the PGM pattern is revealed not only in its lifelong retention, but also in its concentrated expression. It seems that it is not sufficient for us to distribute PGM over a wide range of our movement, we are also obliged to choose – usually unconsciously – behaviour designed purely for its maximum expression. Such behaviour has no other end than the expression of our personality, and is repetitive. Consequently, particular individuals develop characteristic mannerisms. One drums his fingers, another twists a lock of hair, another bites his nails, and yet another pushes his glasses up and down his nose. In movement of this type the particular significance for the individual does not lie in the choice of movement, but in the manner of its performance. There are hundreds of other people who drum, twist, bite or push; what is not shared is the exact pattern of movement, which, as Buchan realized, completely characterizes the individual.

This is particularly obvious when the utility of the action is minimal or non-existent, as in mannerisms, or trivial acts. Asked to observe her husband's manner of winding and setting his alarm clock at night, a woman found that this involved an elaborate and exactly repeated ritual. Changing this made him uneasy, while obstructing it, by wind-

ing it ahead of him, produced real anger and tension, which, in a happy marriage, lasted for days. Although apparently trivial, this ritual was invested with deep significance. If you are prepared to accept the consequences, you can easily think of other experiments which will reveal this, provided that you remember that both the compulsive and the characteristic qualities apply only to movements with PGM. Any carried out with isolated gesture and posture are not the vehicle for significant self-expression.

We have chosen the most concentrated manifestation of the PGM pattern, because here its compulsive qualities are most clearly displayed. However, we distribute PGM throughout many types of bodily behaviour, and must now examine these to establish that the PGM pattern is consistently compulsive in its expression of the personality. Such behaviour falls into three categories:

1 useless or trivial activities,
2 behaviour with grooming purpose,
3 behaviour answering an outside stimulus.

As we have seen, trivial activities are invested with behavioural compulsiveness, and have an importance quite out of proportion to their apparent value. Similarly, grooming activities which are useful, and include necessary forms of body management, are very often invested with concentrated PGM, although unlike our first group they may be carried out of their utility, and are not compulsive by nature. However, the manner in which a person shaves, puts on clothes, takes a bath, brushes his hair, washes, or makes up may be of real personal significance, so that if it were necessary to do the grooming in some other way, there would be a reaction of discomfort, annoyance or

irritability. This probably explains why many people dread the unwelcome intimacy of boarding schools, hospital wards, or staying as guests, and other circumstances where grooming rituals may be upset or exposed to scrutiny. But most people can count on getting away with these activities in privacy and in their own way, so that grooming provides a good opportunity for concentrated PGM expression.

This undercover expression is not available for the third class of activity which includes everything from smoking to eating, from opening doors to shutting windows, from shopping to sunbathing, and from crossing the road to turning the pages of a magazine, in reaction to heat, cold, hunger, indolence, curiosity, or the clock. We do not normally think of our ways of picking a magazine from a news stand, or stretching out on the beach, or miming defiance on a road crossing as particularly expressive of our personalities nor, unless they are in some way extreme, do we think of them as compulsive. But the fact is that the way we do these actions is peculiarly our own, and parts of it are the vehicle for concentrated and compulsive PGM. This is much clearer to most of us when we are watching the movement of others, and most devotees of a sport can tell at once which of the player's movements are of this type. At Wimbledon the serving and returning of tennis balls is essential to the game, and the object of each player is entirely utilitarian. For the onlooker, however, the manner of doing this will absolutely characterize the player. One will bounce the ball four times with decreasing force before serving, another will settle to serve with two hitches of his shirt, while the receiver will prepare for the expected serve with three revolutions of the racquet, a swing of the hips, and four quick jumps. Similarly, on the cricket pitch, a bowler will perform his own war-dance before delivery, while a golfer will trace characteristic patterns with his club as he addresses the ball. All these movements have a ritualistic quality in that they are repetitive and compulsive. They are also, despite the public situation, felt by the performer to be private in a way that underlines their deep personal significance.

These repetitive, compulsive and personal qualities in the concentrated exhibition of PGM provide the perfect basis for mimicry, caricature, and take-offs of the Mike Yarwood variety. It is so characteristic of someone in the public eye to rub his chin just so before answering a question, or to rise up and down on his toes as he makes a point, or to fidget in exactly such and such a manner that the merest suggestion of such a movement indicates to millions the identity of its author. It is also very amusing that we can be so aware of the PGM expression of others, which they feel to be so very private – until we ourselves are exposed to ridicule in this way. We like our own PGM expression to remain private. If mimicked beyond a certain point we easily lose our tempers, and regard it as a personal attack, acknowledging our vulnerability. We all know that in this sort of movement we reveal personality involuntarily, and do not like being caught out. This explains the way in which dislike is often directed towards mannerisms. These body movements say in concentrated way 'This is me'. If anyone dislikes this 'me' then the mannerisms arouse hostility. It is a well-known gag that marriage breakdown can turn on something as trivial as the mismanagement of toothpaste.

In fact there is nothing trivial or unimportant about the concentrated exhibition of PGM. On the contrary, it is here that a person is most himself, and from these movements he derives particular satisfaction. They make him feel good, and if forced to perform the action otherwise, although perhaps in a manner agreed to be more graceful or socially acceptable, he becomes awkward and uncomfortable. A pianist unable to settle to the piano to perform in the concert hall in his own way, which he felt was unsuitable to public appearance, found he was also unable to play to his satisfaction. Analysis of his method showed it to be out of keeping with his PGM, and it was not until a new method was adopted, that was both socially acceptable and in line with his PGM, that he felt he could give his best performance. Similarly, a manager adopted a managerial style which made him the butt of his work force, who arranged to obstruct his dignified entrances, but the amusement died away when he was able to inspect his works in a manner in accord with his PGM, while he himself was able to relax. These men were in stress because they were acting out of line with the PGM compulsion.

The PGM pattern contains in fact the compulsive and concentrated expression of individual personality. It has deep personal significance, and decides what behaviour is right for each person. Any activity in which a person is free to exhibit PGM is more suitable for him than another in which he cannot. In fact there is not usually such polarity, but rather a scale of rightness depending on the degree of free expression. Generally speaking an executive will be regarded as a natural leader if his work allows the expression of PGM, and a worry-guts if it does not; a dentist's clientele will be patients if the movements he needs to make fall within his PGM pattern and martyrs if they do not; we shall enjoy the concert if a musician plays in his own way, and we will sleep best if no one interferes with our alarm clocks or other PGM vehicle!

PGM and prediction: motivation and creative choice

The compulsive nature of the PGM pattern allows even the casual observer to predict behaviour. A wife will know that her husband will clear his throat before answering the phone, or miss a particular step in the stairs. It is most predictable and most concentrated because here it becomes ritualistic. For the more highly trained observer much more is predictable, since a person will respond to a given situation in a particular way. The response is conditioned so that the same reaction is elicited every time the situation arises, providing a rational basis for such T.V. programmes as *Mr and Mrs*, where marriage partners are asked to predict each other's probable responses to certain circumstances. This predictability of behaviour applies not only in small matters, but to the normal demands of daily living, such as the necessity to get up and go to work. Every individual will tackle these tasks differently, but for each person there will be a degree of predictability about the way he will carry them out. Someone was unable to leave for work on time, but he could achieve punctuality by deliberately setting his clock fast, and so triggering his departure, since this was not realistic but ritualistic. The man whose ritual for going to work included a quick run down the garden path, where he snatched a cup of coffee and toast from his particular Jeeves at the gate, did this even though it cannot always have been necessary! Whether late or on time, his response to leaving for work was always the same and triggered this action-sequence. For both men, a link had been established between situation and activity.

Such predictable responses are the opportunity for much teasing and baiting. People instinctively look for the PGM patterns of others, and delight in creating the situations that elicit the expected reaction, knowing that so and so will stiffen his shoulders until this gesture merges into a hunched posture if he is annoyed, or that embarassment will cause a certain facial grimace to merge into a particular wriggle, or that someone will just have to check that the oven is off if rushed from the house. It is no secret that there are pattern links between situations and activities, and there is often an irresistible inclination to exploit this deliberately. In this expectation of an automatic response we are amateur and mischievous disciples of Pavlov's conditioned reflex theory, but with a vital difference of the utmost importance. Pavlov's dogs made no attempt to create the situation that elicited the conditioned response, whereas we not only do this to get at others, but also, more constructively, can ourselves bring about situations which allow us to express our distinctive PGM patterns.

The PGM pattern, then, is a strong motivational force to particular behaviour. It has to be expressed; we can repress it, but not all the time, and so have an inbuilt compulsion to arrange our environment and circumstances for its expression. We know this from our own experience. If someone is a ball of fire, we can reasonably expect him to look for a situation requiring a blaze. Yet we ask such people to cultivate serenity and calm down, when we should rather be helping them to light the right fire! Teachers, faced with pupils with histrionic natures are inclined to bewail their lack of order and method, instead of directing them to the nearest stage; parents with methodical children who would make excellent diamond sorters, china restorers or followers of any vocation requiring concentrated attention over a small span, urge them to become managing directors where attention must be wide-ranging, and a specialization left to others; and we ourselves select goals that it is not in our capacity to achieve. If we insist on ignoring our PGM patterns in this way, we get square pegs in round holes, and, if we persist, we get stress and nervous breakdown and mental hospitals. It makes for as much trouble and as little profit to farm strawberries in the sea as to fish for herrings in the wood. We need to recognize and obey the demands of the PGM pattern. We are not dealing with movements that are trivial and relatively meaningless, as in isolated gesture, but with the means by which a man says 'I am myself'. If he becomes alienated from that self, so that at the bizarre extreme he says 'I am a teapot' – and pours himself out – a situation not unknown to the psychiatrist – then there is serious personality breakdown.

Since the ways in which we can express our PGM may not always be very satisfactory, many rituals and ceremonies are designed to provide a safe and acceptable vehicle for the concentrated expression of our patterns. Where ritual is alive it has the compulsive qualities of PGM expression, but many of our rituals whether folk or religious rites are dead, although participants must once have been fully involved in the movement sequences, investing them with PGM. In the movements of a modern christening ceremony there is neither the precision in the choice of movements nor the compulsive merging of the posture and gesture in their performance that is characteristic of true ritual, and there is likely to be more true ritual outside the church in the greetings exchanged than at the ceremony itself. This contrast was examined in the film *The Godfather*, where a vendetta had been arranged to coincide with the christening of the leader's son. In the church, no one was involved in the ritual, so that the chief's pre-occupation with the Mafia bloodbath did not look unusual, whereas, during the greetings outside, where everyone was involved in social ritual, he was clearly set apart, although his expression had not changed.

The purpose of ritual is to translate feeling into movement of a precise compulsive character, and some of our religious or quasi-religious ceremonies probably do this. Marriage ceremonies, carol-singing and funerals are probably invested with PGM, at least in parts and for some participants, while harvest festivals almost certainly are not. Those that are not are games, routines or formalities rather than rituals, so that people have a solemn ridiculous air that goes with isolated posture and gesture, and the occasion has a routine, tiresome atmosphere, because no deep feeling is present to bring about the merged movement that is so apparent on the exceptional occasions of real public emotion, such as the funeral of President Kennedy. Sadly, many of our social occasions also have little of the spontaneity or compulsiveness that is characteristic of movement performed with PGM. On such occasions, people are too busy keeping up with the Joneses or playing games to reveal themselves to each other, with results that are frustrating, tiring, boring and nonsensical. Official business meetings, too, tend to be gestural, in marked contrast to the revelatory movements of the prior caballings and groupings. Sports ceremonies, however, give more consistent opportunities for PGM performances because of the deep feelings involved.

It is not, however, correct to say that the presence or absence of deep feeling decides when movements are invested with PGM and

when they are not. It is possible to feel deeply on religious matters and yet to carry out religious ceremonies and rituals with isolated posturing and gesturing, and it is possible to invest the trivial winding of a clock with PGM. The importance of ritual lies in its potentiality as a vehicle for PGM expression. Either we must express concentrated PGM in public, or we must do so in private. If we cannot ritualize in church or folk dance, we will do so with our razors or lipsticks. There is an immense diversity of individual expression in man, so that his compelling drives can be expressed in many varied ways, becoming significant or insignificant in so far as they are invested with PGM. The spate of books published during the last decade comparing man's behaviour with that of animals has only limited importance for the behavioural field because the comparison exposes the common primary drives of men and animals, but ignores the vastly different social structure in which we live and behave. We may have sexual drives like apes, covet territory like robins, or destroy competitors like wolves, but the way in which we express these drives is another matter. We are compelled to act out our PGM patterns, but we also choose the circumstances in which we act.

The PGM pattern's importance for research lies in the link it creates between opposing behaviourist schools of thought. On the one hand, the Skinner–Pavlov school emphasizes the importance of conditioning as the determinant of behaviour. Maslow, on the other hand, says that a hierarchy of human needs motivates behaviour. This school asserts that we must be free from stress occasioned by hunger, domestic problems, and crises of self-esteem in order to achieve self-actualization. The PGM pattern offers a link between these two theories. It is a mode of self-expression which is achieved most fully when the individual is free from stress, but, when it is not fully understood, we fail to avoid stress and to achieve personal fulfilment. Fortunately, the existence of our distinctive and individual PGM patterns actually conditions us to seek situations in which we can achieve such fulfilment. If we learn really to understand our PGM patterns, we can assist such conditioning by making creative choices wisely according to our circumstances. In this way we can achieve harmony with ourselves, and make a more creative contribution to the community. We can do this if we examine our PGM patterns to see who we are, and put our findings into words. It is time to decode the secret language of movement.

8

The meaning of movement in words

Everybody from duke to dustman, from princess to passion-flower cries aloud in their movements 'I am myself!' If you wish to answer the question 'Who am I?', or 'Who is he?', you have only to listen to this speaking silence in the right way, and the right way to listen to movement is to understand the rationale for the methods of observation outlined in this book, and to use them. It is essential that the suggested experiments are carried out, because any book that offers a practical technique, whether a cookbook, a music manual, or an exploration into behaviour suffers from an inherent problem – its inevitable distance from direct experience. Only you, the reader, can carry out cookbook recipes so that you actually taste and smell the dish, or play an instrument, or attend the opera, so that you actually make or hear the music, and only you can observe movement in a way that enables you to understand behaviour. This book – any book – can only tell you how to set about it. You must try it for yourself. What this book can do is to explain as clearly as possible how you can understand the self-expression that is conveyed through the PGM patterns, whether your own or others.

The simplest foundation on which to build an explicit understanding of the PGM pattern is the three-stage theory of action, which postulates that, in the initiation of any new movement, three distinct stages must be worked through. First, no action can be initiated without the direction of *attention*. Attention must be given in a particular direction as an indispensable first stage, although this is not in itself adequate to bring an action into being. Second, there must be *intention* to act, otherwise the attention fades into passivity. Lastly, there must be a *commitment* to action arising from the intention. If any one of these stages is missing action does not arise. Movement can be visualized as a cloth woven of three threads: attention, intention, and commitment. From these, different personalities weave a variety of self-expression patterns in non-verbal behaviour. This theory of action is our way of tuning in to the secret language of movement and our method for the translation of this movement into words. If we could not effect such a translation of movement into words there would be no point in the many words in this book; they would all have been wasted! But beyond doubt movement can be put into words, giving explicit expression to the non-verbal expression of the personality that we have been studying. We have only to pay attention!

Paying attention

The demand, 'Pay attention', is familiar to us all from childhood, and so also are the gestures that normally accompany it. A beckoning gesture usually consists of a quick tilt of the head, or an upwards movement of the hand, with an outstretched index finger. Anyone seeing such a gesture, or one of its many variations, will interpret this as a signal meaning, 'I want your attention'. Not that we necessarily react as the beckoner would wish! That all depends on the circumstances. We may have something much more interesting on hand, and may be too preoccupied to react at all, especially if we only just

perceive the gesture out of the corner of one eye. We could easily ignore it altogether, but maybe we acknowledge it with a gesture glance that signals 'All right, all right! I'm busy for heaven's sake, but I'll get round to it in a minute!' All this can be acted out in gesture only language, although if the beckoner sees us receive the signal head on as it were, and sees us deliberately ignore it, it is unlikely that the silent language will be confined to gesture for long! If the beckoning has to be repeated, and the beckoner becomes increasingly desperate or determined to gain your attention, there will be an inevitable transition from gesture to posture movement. Further, if the beckoning is seconded by an expression of annoyance intended to force your attention, your own posture movement will also become involved. A gesture of the mime-type will have become translated into PGM to create a more highly charged and significant interaction between you and the other person. *Pay attention* is being shouted, however silently, and, whether you like it or not, a state of attentiveness exists, even if you go on trying your best to ignore everything. The very ignoring *is* itself attentiveness. Good examples of this come from every classroom. 'I'm sure he's deaf', fretted the teacher to the parents of one small boy, 'He never hears a word in class!' The surprised parents hurried him to the doctor, a practical man with a strong sense of humour. Directing the child to a distant door, he whispered an almost inaudible 'Stop!' The boy's instant obedience ended the consultation. On the way home, the child was confidential. 'I don't like my teacher', he remarked. 'I get ever so tired not hearing what she says!' Attending to his infant cure for boring teachers was costing him a lot of energy.

Such apparent inattentiveness often results in annoyance and is described by onlookers in such phrases as, 'If looks could kill . . .', or, 'You could have cut the air with a knife!' There is a whole family of gestures and postures which aims to attain, maintain or provoke attention. We all both perform and recognize them. However, some of us perform or recognize them better than others. Obviously, like the boy at school, we are more likely to give attention where we are interested, and when we are not otherwise occupied. If the boy at school had not been bored he might have been attentive; he was not necessarily inattentive by nature. All the same, many people are inattentive by nature and are recognizable as children who are inattentive in class, teenagers who cannot take a hint, husbands who do not notice new hairstyles or clothes, women who 'never see a soul I know' when shopping, managers who do not notice a bad atmosphere among

staff, and so on. In such people, the springs of action are partly
stopped up because giving attention, or responding to claims on our
attention, is a logical first stage in any action process. How can we
possibly fulfil anything to which we have not given some attention in
the first place?

Suppose that we are, right now, giving attention to this book. Only
two things can follow on:

1 We drop it – we are disinterested. Even so, some aspect of it may
remain in the memory and pop up again later.

2 We continue to give it attention – and move on to the next stage.
Obviously for action to arise there has to be a next stage. No action is
accomplished by giving attention. There may of course be a great deal
of mental 'activity'; but this is using the word 'action' to mean something outside of the physical, motor, action to which we are applying it
in this book. No physical action is accomplished purely by giving
attention, but it is an indispensable first stage. We should be very
surprised if a sergeant-major were to bring his men to attention with
the usual powerful bellow, and then leave them there. We expect
something to follow on from his roar. 'A--tten---tion!' We spring into

readiness. Something is about to happen. Attention to something. We are about to see some action!

Intention: get ready! Get set!

Unfortunately, we are making assumptions. We are assuming that attention can lead straight into action. But this is not so. There is really no reason why the sergeant-major should not leave his men in a state of attentiveness. In fact, if there is to be a parade-ground inspection, that is exactly what he will do. The squad will have to remain in the attentive state until they are ordered to relax and stand at ease. They will do this with relief, because this is not really the expected course of events. What is automatically expected is some instruction which conveys an intention to the whole group such as 'By the left, quick . . .' which, if action is to be generated, brings everyone to the identical intention to take this particular action – marching – at the same moment. The daydreaming young recruit who fails to achieve this state of intention on the command will receive the full blast of the sergeant-major's intention in a way that will dismiss all other attentions from his mind.

Fortunately, you do not need to join the army to study intention, and need not risk the sergeant-major's wrath. If, in civilian life, we give attention to someone, and find that he is gritting his teeth, clenching his fists, or stamping his feet, we do not interpret such movements as expressive of attention, but as evidence of some intention towards us. Our reaction will not be, 'Do you want me?' but, 'What in the world is bothering *you*'. If such gestures get to the PGM stage, so that the teeth gritting is backed up by total body-tension, and the clenched fist or stamping foot has the pressure or the weight of the whole body behind it, we are likely to read this as more than a mere signal and feel that something is about to happen! We would react by getting ready to back away, duck or sidestep, because the gestures and postures we see are ones which invariably have a distinct pressurizing quality. The pressure of such gestures and postures or intention may be strong or light. The statement 'I insist', may be accompanied by a light finger touch, and still convey as much intensity or intention as a strong thump of the fist – how the intention is conveyed will depend on cultural and other conditioning factors. We may prefer the prod to the thump, but either way when we see, or feel, the pressurizing in the

PGM, we shall feel that there is some expression of conviction, threat or intent. We still cannot know what is intended to happen – but we do know that our companion is not just attracting our attention, but is letting us know that he intends something to happen.

A little everyday observation will soon show you many examples of gestures and postures or attention resolving into gestures and postures of intention, although sometimes they may occur so quickly as to be difficult to analyse. For instance, if I scream in agony as I trip and roll downstairs, I would hope that your response of giving attention would be overlapped, within a fraction of a second, by the expression of intention to do something about it. You would have to be very callous to settle your elbows on the banister rail, and settle down to give your full attention to viewing the disaster. Most people in such a situation would be spurred from the attention to the intention stage, but this need not happen, especially in less extreme cases. It is one of the most usual objections put forward by critics of television that constant viewing of all sorts of disasters from the safety of an armchair and a TV supper blunts the transition process from attention to intention. After a while, it is argued, the habit of arresting the action process before it reaches the intention stage prevents us taking the next step towards doing something about the outside world. In recent years, a variety of experiments have been conducted to examine the causes of failure to make this transition. It seems that, in high-density cities, people become conditioned to expect the 'proper' person to take action, so that murder, rape, robbery or torture can take place before their eyes without them feeling personally spurred to action. This, however, is due to conditioning and not to the nature of the per-sonality, but there are people who are lacking in intention, and these are characterized by a tendency to be spectators, to stand well back, to be vague or distrait or unpunctual. They have the same characteristics as T. S. Eliot's cat, Macavity – the cat who was never *there*.

Obviously, if you see a ball – or a person – roll down the stairs and you do not form the intention to move into action, your attention comes to nothing and no action can follow. On the other hand, we may give ourselves the civilian equivalent of the sergeant-major's 'By the left, quick . . .', and our muscles will respond by tensing into the state of intention – a state particularly recommended to a new recruit! At last we shall see action. Something is going to happen!

Commitment: go man go!

Once again we are making assumptions. Imagine, for instance, that the sergeant-major is shot dead before he can utter the word 'March', or he succumbs to sunstroke, or the prayers of the new recruit are answered and he is struck by lightning, or some bolt from the blue which prevents the utterance of the final word of command. Then there is no doubt that, however the squad reacts, it will not be with a brisk left foot forward. Another stage is needed to initiate action, and this is commitment. If the sergeant-major had forced out the word 'March', then the squad would have made that act of commitment, and nothing on earth, or from the skies, could have prevented the imple-mentation of that action, no matter how quickly it had afterwards been called off. Action is triggered with the act of commitment.

In an earlier chapter we considered the slight gesture necessary to secure a purchase at auction. A nod will often be sufficient. The attention to what is being sold and the intention to buy the lot will have been essential preliminaries, but it is the nod that is taken as the commitment to buy. As we see someone tensing his muscles for the nod, we know that he is on the brink of doing something. He is on his marks in the same sense as an athlete waiting for the starting gun. Once he nods, or makes any other act of commitment, then life is never quite the same again. The action is in being. Acts of attention and intention can lapse without changing the situation, but acts of commitment are the end of the sequence and start an implementation process that makes the original situation impossible to recover. If the sergeant-major shouts 'March' and drops dead, the immediate cry of 'Halt' from the quick-witted second-in-command will not prevent the implementation of marching but only limit its duration. The squad will need to make a new commitment to stop, and this second commitment cannot wipe out the effect of the first. Commitment is in fact irrevocable – and this is what is often dodged. 'He means well but he never gets anything done' is a typical comment on someone who calls off action at the commitment stage.

There is no need to join the army to see commitment in action sequences, or indeed to relate it to an activity as positive as marching. Most of us are lucky enough to be offered a cup of coffee in the course of the day, and ungrateful enough to take it for granted. When someone asks, 'Do you want a cup of coffee?', we might commit ourselves to drinking it with a slight nod, barely pausing at the preceding attention and intention stages, especially if the question and answer were part of a daily ritual. However, if the enthusiasm of the coffee-maker suddenly evaporates or there is a power cut, the question may change to, 'Will you have iced coffee or whisky?' in which case we will probably respond with action expressive of attention and intention, rather than commitment, and our PGM would convey our surprise, annoyance, interest or amusement. Commitment would be delayed. If the coffee-maker has reached the end of his tether, the question might be, 'Why don't we go and get plastered?', and our reaction, whether outraged or delighted, is likely to involve PGM expressive of attention, intention and commitment in sequence, since the unexpectedness of it will arouse attention, and the exaggerated nature of the proposed solution would compel a full response.

Energy and three-stage action

Our movement can be understood as a constant interplay of attention, intention and commitment, overlapping at many different levels, and over varying time spans. Study of PGM behaviour has shown that different individuals energize these action-stages in different proportions. When behaviour samples provide valid bases for comparison, we find, say, that John energizes his behaviour 60 per cent towards attention, 30 per cent towards intention and only 10 per cent towards commitment, whereas Jill energizes her behaviour only 10 per cent towards attention, 30 per cent towards intention, and 60 per cent towards commitment, while their favourite aunt energizes attention 30 per cent, intention 60 per cent and commitment 10 per cent.

	Attention	Intention	Commitment
John	60%	30%	10%
Jill	10%	30%	60%
Aunt	30%	60%	10%

It is easy to see from this that their behaviour will be radically different in identical situations. John has grown up with a PGM pattern which causes him to act attentively in a new situation, whereas Jill has a pattern which makes her rush into commitment, while the aunt knows just what ought to be done and spends her time organizing to get to grips with things.

Imagine that this ill-assorted crew are abandoned on a desert island. John is delighted. Obviously he must measure the land and take soundings around the coast, note the vegetation, look up his copies of *Robinson Crusoe* and *Swiss Family Robinson*! Reviewing, surveying, exploring and researching the situation keeps him busy until nightfall, by which time he has formed the intention of building camp in a certain spot – but has missed the opportunity to carry out his plan. Jill, meanwhile, cannot wait to know where she is, and settles at once to make camp where they land, without taking time to appreciate that the spot is damp, infested with insects, and as far as possible from the only water supply. Meanwhile, the aunt, intending to put in for a permanent billing as Girl Friday, has laid out the equipment in best Girl Guide style, drawn up a schedule of their immediate needs and the desirable requirements for a camp site, but cannot quite bring herself to start making camp. Fortunately, they are all aware of their

different PGM patterns and so they survive very nicely. Jill takes John's report on the island into account, accepts the aunt's assessment of the practicalities and mobilizes her organization. Then she gets the camping process into action just as John returns from a further exploration, and the aunt starts to plan the next day's activities.

We are not much concerned with their future adventures, but what is apparent is that their behaviour in the face of the new situation could be predicted from a study of their individual PGM patterns, and both their strengths and weaknesses in the situation assessed. Obviously, a highly committed person like Jill is likely to make her worst mistakes soon after arrival at the island, when the situation is unexplored, and headlong commitment to unknown and uninvestigated plans for survival might have disastrous consequences. On the other hand, she is the only person who can actually pick up the mallet and hammer home the tent pegs to keep them all from death through exposure. Clearly, the sooner she is in a situation where John has got his information about the island highly systematized, the more effective and the less dangerous her qualities will become. John, meanwhile, does not have a hope of surviving without her, because he will die inadvertently, almost, from cold, or thirst, or fever, while making his fascinating enquiries into the nature of desert islands. *If* he survives, however, it is his book that is going to be a bestseller, or uncover some new breakthrough in knowledge. Meantime his qualities, from the point of view of the island band, are most likely to be useful for long-term survival, when the situation does not call for rapid and opportunist commitment to action against the odds. Throughout the adventure, the invaluable aunt keeps low spirits and pessimism at bay by the force of her intention to win out in their new surroundings, and by her power to organize all available resources to this end. Nothing daunts her! Unlike John, she does not enquire whether earthquake, tempest, or fire might interfere with her plans. It is enough for her to lay hands on immediate necessities and to overcome immediate obstacles. Plans, procedures and organization are her forte – but she stops short of picking up the mallet. Their first night's survival or destruction must largely depend on Jill's commitment – and luck. If she makes the right snap decision although on too little evidence and without proper plans procedure and organization, they stand a chance. They should make a good team if they survive the start!

Acting out a pattern

We can understand why people behave the way they do much better when we realize that they are acting out a prevailing pattern. We shall not waste time handing the mallet to John or asking Jill to undertake exploration, and we shall not expect the aunt to achieve results from her plans and organization. We know that it is Jill who will benefit from this work preparation when she takes action.

Of course, on a desert island, the likelihood is that everyone will be relatively uninhibited in seeking to tackle the situation by acting out his own pattern, whereas the expression and effect of the individual pattern is usually subject to a variety of conditioning influences. Cultural, social, and parental conditioning affects gestures only, but must be taken into account, and a person may attempt to condition himself by consciously allowing for, or a commitment-oriented person may try to avoid, acting in blind haste, or may seek work where controls have been set up to minimize errors in this direction.

All the same, the PGM pattern is always there, and not only there but exercising a strong motivational influence. Put a strongly attention-oriented person, like John, into any situation alongside a commitment-oriented person, like Jill, and, given equal responsibility, they will act in contrasting ways and styles. If the situation includes an area of muddle on the one hand, and an area where the way ahead is clear, then their different styles will show a stark contrast. John, and other similarly attention-oriented people, will concentrate on the muddle. They will be quite unable to tolerate doing nothing about it because of the opportunities it presents for research, survey, definition and clarification, they will neglect the 'clear ahead' area, and may miss some excellent opportunities. The commitment-oriented person, meanwhile, will join Jill in the 'clear ahead' area, the 'all systems go' signal finding an immediate response in their patterns. They will neglect the muddle, or make it so much worse under their leadership that progress in the 'clear ahead' area is undermined. Meanwhile, the intention-oriented aunts, and kindred spirits, will be picking out the most challenging issue and pursuing it determinedly through thick and thin, even after it becomes patently clear that it would be much better to give it up, and concentrate on something else.

The wide variety of ways in which attention, intention and commitment may be present in the individual PGM pattern accounts for the fascinating conflict and diversity of personalities in daily living, the richly varied response to situations in history, and, in perceptive hands, for some of the most vital characterization in books. Two classics, familiar to most of us from childhood, clearly portray differing types of PGM pattern in action. In Kenneth Grahame's *Wind in the Willows*, Rat and Badger are commitment-oriented, and the action in the book springs from them. Mole is attention-oriented. He sees and hears every weird tree, every creak and patter in the Wild Wood, and every pattern of the snow, but he draws no practical conclusion from the discovery of a doormat; it is Rat who unearths the door, and bundles him over the threshold, half dead from exposure. Meanwhile, the wayward Toad conceives one stubborn intention after another, but, having organized a canary-yellow caravan, an expensive limousine, a daring escape, or a humiliating, but most necessary, barge trip in disguise, proves quite incapable of pursuing the action-sequence through the commitment stage. He wrecks the caravan, drives recklessly into the arms of the law, cannot support the role of washerwoman, and unwisely taunts policemen. In A. A. Milne's *House at Pooh Corner*, Pooh is always at the attention stage, Rabbit is for ever organizing – but not achieving action, and Kanga and Tigger make things happen.

Now, the motivational pull of the PGM pattern is so strong that, where individual styles can be indulged, people who are oriented primarily to attention, or intention, or commitment not only take every opportunity of acting out their patterns, but actually seek out and create the circumstances which allow them to do so. An attention-oriented person will find a need for research activity in the most unlikely places, and dig up muddles to investigate over and above the call of duty, so that it is probable that Pooh is still composing ditties and counting honey pots, while Mole is enchanted by spring into forgetting whitewash and groceries. Similarly, the commitment-oriented person will create opportunities for competitive exploitation whether it is desirable or not, regardless of the wealth or security he may already have achieved. It is not as unreasonable as it sounds to describe a millionaire's wealth as his biggest problem, as potentially frustrating as a butter mountain might be to a passionate producer of dairy gold. Can anyone doubt that Kanga is still administering Strengthening Medicine, or that the Rats and Badgers have continued to create confrontations with the Stoats and Weasels of Berkshire? Again the intention-oriented person will find obstacles and challenges where none need exist; no doubt A. A. Milne's Rabbit has not run out of lost relations, and is organizing new expeditions to the North Pole. Why, in Aesop's brilliant fable of Tortoise and Hare, did Hare leave his slow and steady, but utterly committed, challenger to win the race? If he had not been so greatly intention-oriented and so little committed, he must surely have taken a snooze after, rather than before, the race. Such powerful motivations can be assessed from the PGM pattern, and their effects predicted, provided always that allowance is

made for constraints in the situation which prevent full PGM expression – a large but not invalidating qualification.

You can now look around you and try to classify behaviour using the three-stage-action scheme. Is your brother or sister, colleague or friend exasperating you by letting opportunities go by, while constantly giving ideas to others from which he or she does not benefit? Are you kept on the hop by an employer, or spouse, or child who cannot relax and enjoy a well-organized and comfortable situation, but has to find some front or cliff-face to attack? Are you green with envy because a friend gets away with the sort of daring and opportunist actions that would land you in jail or your coffin, if you were to copy them? If so, you will now easily understand such exasperating, daunting or amazing behaviour from what you know of the attention–intention–commitment patterns of the people concerned. You will find that most people are definitely oriented in some directions and not in others, and you will be wondering what has happened to the well-balanced person whose attention–intention–commitment orientation is energized $33\frac{1}{3}$ per cent towards each.

This ideal and self-sufficient man or woman is attractive in theory, but rarely seems to exist in real life. When such people are found, as they are from time to time, the perfect motivational balance works out rather differently in practice to what you might expect. Just as a pair of scissors, perfectly made, will not cut, so a complete balance in motivation brings a certain ineffectiveness in action. The cancelling out of motivations results in immobility, boxing the personality into a square. It is as though you were watching one of the toy clowns that are made with a weight in the rounded base; whichever way it is pushed, it returns to its original position. Activity requires imbalance, and studies show that such imbalance is normal in the personality. Consequently, we all need others to complement and balance our own qualities.

If you can understand what these are, and learn to assess your own PGM pattern, you will be much better at choosing your boss, or colleague, or husband, or wife, or friends, and generally exercising discretion in relationships, because you are using a sound basis for your choices. Unfortunately, the advice 'Know thyself', is as difficult to apply here as elsewhere, and it would seem that we are much better at assessing the motivational drives of others than at understanding our own. Still, we do gain such insights, and our knowledge of others is valuable too. When a task requires the co-operation of several people with different PGM patterns, we can learn to judge whether a particular team will work well together, or produce hopeless conflict, and we can influence choices in a constructive way.

Assertion and perspective

Our chances of making correct judgments on the motivations of ourselves and others will be very much improved, if we add another dimension to our three-stage-action concept. We must now draw a distinction between assertion and perspective. Suppose someone holds out a box of chocolates in your direction, or maybe a bottle of brandy shouting, 'Who wants this?' As you lunge forward, or make a grab – whether gesture or posture does not matter – you realize that you may lose your balance. In the fraction of a second available, you have to decide whether to carry through your assertive grab for the goodies and risk falling flat on your face, or whether to regain your balanced perspective and risk losing out. All things being equal, some

people will decide one way and some the other. You may not know which you would do, but generally speaking the moment of truth takes us by surprise! Whether you got the chocolates or brandy, or missed them, you will not have missed the significance of the illustration for posture and gesture, for here are two processes which may be in affinity and complement each other, or may be diverse and work in opposite directions. These are the assertion and perspective processes – the process of asserting effort, without which there can be no movement, and the process of maintaining perspective without which we would surrender our sense of balance and fail to attain the object of movement. These two processes are clearly distinguishable in posture and gesture, although practice is needed in observing them with any degree of accuracy. These processes can now be linked to the three-stage-action theory we have already considered.

The assertion–perspective processes and three-stage action

Attention = investigation or exploration

If we *assert* attention, then we are motivated to search, probe, get more information, analyse, dissect, and generally pursue a detective-style procedure. This is the 'Elementary my dear Watson!' style that eventually provoked the creator of Sherlock Holmes to fling him from a precipice, but inspired the admirers of the investigator-extra-ordinary to insist on his return from the crevasse. Whether you personally like or hate investigators, the prominence in literature of

Sexton Blake or of the snappy Hercule Poirot, or the imperturbable Lord Peter Wimsey, or the TV fame of the wheelchair wonder, Ironside, shows how easily we recognize the classic investigator, and the nature of investigating activity. It has a clear-cut simplicity which is shared by its archetypal exponents.

This is much less apparent when the main object is to maintain *perspective* in attention. Whereas it is almost impossible to imagine Holmes far from the scene of the crime or the latest clue, the person maintaining perspective attentively will actually seek to be at a distance, in order to be better placed to gather up a number of threads, and to enhance his or her receptivity to the whole scene. Here you have sheet, instead of fork, lightning which will fill the whole sky with light, rather than strike upon distinct points. This is attention of the exploratory type, and involves reviewing, combining, selecting and seeing all round the situation. Flora in *Cold Comfort Farm* was a good explorer. She refused to give specific attention to any one of the curiosities and oddities with which she was confronted, withdrew to a neat base of her own and proceeded to put the comfortless world into perspective by combining personalities in the best possible way. She singled out the prime doom-maker in spite of appearances to the contrary, finally homing in on Aunt Ada, who had seen something nasty in the woodshed, before sending her off into the wide blue yonder.

In the attention stage, there is a world of difference between a good investigator, and a good explorer. The investigator tends to be narrowly confined in his attentiveness, while the explorer employs his far and wide. Neither trait is good or bad in itself. It all depends on the circumstances, and the end desired. For instance, you can imagine how Holmes would have been cramped in style if he had felt obliged to consider the possible effects on his criminals of bringing them to justice, or the ins and outs of his relationship with Watson, or the best devices for surviving falls from precipices. You immediately have him at check instead of hallooing in the hunt. On the other hand, imagine the results of subjecting Gibbon to a battery of questions of the 'What did he have for breakfast?' type, while begging him to confine his attention to local history. You may not admire his work but at least it is there to be ignored! You can easily think of other books where the attentiveness displayed is of the exploratory type. There is Tolkien's *Lord of the Rings*, or there is Jane Austen's work, or there is *Gone with the Wind*. All these books have explorer authors, attracted by the panoramic view, where, say, an archivist must be concerned with the nitty-gritty.

Obviously, then, if you give a project to a good investigator, who is a poor explorer, he will exhaustively examine it, define each part, meticulously note detail, and exclude all other matters while doing so. He is just the man to sort out bits of broken archaeological treasures, or sift evidence on a dig, or analyse the composition of the soil or whatever. The explorer in such projects will behave quite differently, looking up the history of ancient pots in general, writing articles on the similarity of the dig with a previous project elsewhere, or deciding to offer the Third World a new scheme of agriculture devised for particular soils, which he will be sure to have someone else, probably an investigator, analyse for him.

On a project together, the investigator and the explorer may so deploy their diverse attention styles as to utterly stultify each other. The explorer comes up with a general picture of affairs and an overall view of what ought to be done; the investigator immediately raises a thousand detailed objections, stressing the explorer's carelessness in overlooking them. Or, the investigator presents a detailed solution to a problem, and the explorer blandly dismisses it as unsuited to the general scheme of things and a lot of fuss about nothing. It is hard to imagine Sherlock Holmes and Tolkien travelling hand in hand! But, if each understands the other's strengths, so that both skills may be deployed, they may make a formidable team. Who could doubt the success of Agatha Christie's Miss Marple teamed with Jane Austen? Then again, two investigators may profitably share a world of detection and analysis, if the circumstances encourage effort in a narrow field and the ignoring of the wider world. The irascible Holmes and Sexton Blake might enjoy their common motivation, or Archimedes appreciate an introduction to Marie Curie. Similarly, two explorers may enjoy a panoramic view of events if circumstances permit the overlooking of detail. We might team Tolstoy and Balzac, or Gibbon and Toynbee. It all depends on the circumstances, and the chosen goal, but it is certain that in the realistic choices of everyday living, a proper understanding of differing attention motivations can greatly improve our development of skills and choice of colleagues to achieve desired ends and solve problems.

Intention = determination or confrontation

If we assert intention, the second of our three stages in the theory of action we adopt the typical traits of the 'go-getter'. What ever attracts the 'go-getter's' attention becomes the object of his resolution to 'get on with it', to get it, to achieve it, and so on, without letting anything stand in the way, so that a conclusion is reached at the earliest possible moment. Industrial tycoons are usually depicted as intention-asserters. 'Get me onto him, at *once*' they grit out from behind a teeth-chomped cigar, 'Leave it with me', they command. 'Get outa my way boy', they steamroller associates, leaving admirers gasping at their determination, and detractors infuriated at being pushed aside. Determination is the keynote of asserted intention.

Much less drama is generated when someone sets out to maintain perspective in expressing intention. This is because his motivation appears less personal. He is concerned to take a situation 'fair and square', 'take it on the chin', 'measure up to things'. It seems that the intended end is assessed as desirable, so that the issue is made to stand out in relief. Here, you feel, is a warrior woman determined not to evade the issue, or a man dauntless in the face of compelling demands. You call to mind, not so much Top Cat, or Deputy Dawg but Horatius on the bridge, or the frog who swam in the bowl of cream until he had churned it to butter, or the boy with his finger in the dyke, or Canute facing the oncoming waves. What you see is not so much determination as confrontation. There is a different quality in the intention of the confronter to that of the determined man. Like the difference between the investigator and the explorer, there is a difference in scope and intensity. Mr Determination is the fork lightning, and Mrs Confrontation the sheet flash. He is all push and fire and pestilence, she is blocking, resisting, pressurizing, enduring. His danger is that he may force the issue at the wrong point and exhaust his firepower on the wrong target, hers that she will fail to see a weak spot develop and be left holding the bridge against an army that is busy swimming the river. Combined, they should exert a great force on the situation, opposed, they will probably fall out over timing and methods.

Obviously, if the issue is limited and the goal clear, the determined man is the person to push matters to a conclusion, to get to grips with the problem to resolve on appropriate action. You have a blueprint for the Caesar of Latin textbooks. 'Caesar, having made camp, decided to attack the Gauls', and, of course, show them who was who! On the other hand, it is no accident that we think of confrontation as descriptive of picket lines and sieges, expeditions to Everest, marches and rallies, armies making a stand, neighbours arms akimbo. It is not so much a matter of knocking a hole in the wall as of slowly, relentlessly deploying a force that will push it over. There is a gathering of forces, a linking of arms, a surge forward, rather than a call to charge into the breach, or a rush of commands, or a stream of international cables.

Commitment = decision or anticipation

The same dichotomy holds good in the third stage of our action–theory – commitment. If we assert commitment, we are intent on making the best possible tactical or opportunist use of time – even if this involves waiting for the right moment, rather than quickly seizing an opportunity. It is the rightness of decision that is given priority, and since a badly timed decision is a wrong decision, our activity is one of *deciding*. Once again decision has a pointed, gathered connotation and its qualities are those of fork, rather than sheet, lightning. You have the accuracy of the parachute jump, the spring at the start of the race, the split-second leap to safety, with all the action-man qualities of The Saint, or Starsky and Hutch, or Virginia Wade, or Fanny Cradock. 'I made my decision on the spot', they announce, or 'He could always make up his mind', or 'How decisive she is'. On the other hand if you were motivated towards perspective in commitment you would be all the time assessing your new stance in respect to the initiated trend of events and considering the likely outcome or prospect. Your true action-man decides to jump, and that's it. Your perspective-committed free-faller is considering the usefulness of his jump and the change in temperature as he falls. One man jumps, the other is falling, although both are committed to the third stage of action – the parachute jump. Now obviously to win at tennis, or save your skin as The Saint, you would be better off as the decision-maker, but as a politician, or a general, or a company executive more benefit would be derived from anticipation. Once again, the decider catches the moment but may miss the full effect, and the anticipator may mistime his jump while considering his landing.

Here, then, are the six action motivations derived from the three-stage-action theory:

Attention

1 *Investigating* = defining, categorizing, fact-finding, establishing method, defining standards and principles, extracting information in a defined area.
2 *Exploring* = assessing scope of information, looking for alternative possibilities and approaches, questioning assumptions and reasons.

Intention

3 *Determining* = having firmness of purpose; showing determination, persisting against odds; resisting pressure.
4 *Confronting* = crystallizing issues, establishing importance, challenging; recognizing immediate needs realistically; accepting hard facts in a forthright manner.

Commitment

5 *Deciding* = having a sense of timing, setting off action implementation at the right moment, settling timing priorities, seizing opportunities, being good at flexible, on-the-spot programming.
6 *Anticipating* = looking ahead, foreseeing consequences of action, evaluating practicalities, continually anticipating future developments, systematic future planning.

This, then, is the check-list by which you can assess the motivation of others and yourself, and from this assessment determine how an individual is likely to behave in any particular set of circumstances. Your equipment for translating the speaking silence into words is now working, and you have only to decide where to make your first tests.

9

Movement means motivation

From here on matters are in your hands. This book must now become the basis for your own observation of movement in real life. As in a child's pop-up book, the illustrations must rise from the pages, and they must also take on the movement we have been examining, and step out into your daily living. All we can do in this chapter is to recall how we have constructed our kinaesthetic equipment and give it a trial run by working through some examples. These have been selected from hundreds of studies, made by analysing different PGM patterns, and evaluating them in the ways we considered in the last chapter. We call these action profiles and after you have looked at these examples, you will be able to construct your own. You may want to try out kinaesthetic equipment on Aunt Bertha, or the boss, or colleagues, or subordinates, or your friends, or your teachers or your family, but remember that any experimenter worth his salt is also willing to try his experiments on himself!

Your own body movement, like that of everyone you meet, is made up of posturing and gesturing, which merge in PGM to reveal a pattern of action motivation uniquely your own. Like everyone else, you have a pattern for distributing energy in a way that motivates you more to one sort of activity, and less to another. If you observe your own PGM pattern, you can decide for yourself how much you energize the different action stages. You can then draw up an action-profile of yourself that will put this motivation into words.

Unfortunately, if you start out in this way, you may prove yourself an honest experimenter, worth a whole salt mine, and yet land in unexpected difficulties, since the most difficult movement to observe is your own. Unless you have your own Hall of Mirrors, you cannot easily see yourself. You have exactly the same problem as a woman trying to give herself an elaborate hair-do; she would like to take her head off and put it somewhere convenient, and you would like to put your moving body over there so that you can see what it is doing! It would, after all, be better to start with Aunt Bertha while you build up

experience, since she is over there as large as life where you can see her, while you are in your own way, as it were. However, if you want to draw up her action-profile or anyone else's, you should use the same method as your would use on yourself.

First, collect your tools: these are your kinaesthetic sense which enables you to discern the process of movement clearly, and your faculty for discrimination which enables you to distinguish posture from gesture and detect where they merge. Whatever the present level of your skill and perception in observing movement, these tools will enhance them, and practice will bring you unexpected rewards. You have only to acquire some 'feel' for movement to go along with your new understanding of how the PGM pattern works, and you will find that you are looking at your own behaviour and that of others with new eyes. As you observe movement, differentiating between posture and gesture, and building up data on PGM, you will gain confidence, and find that you are automatically discerning the PGM pattern, and categorizing it into the three action stages: attention, intention and commitment. You then have only to make the distinction between assertion and perspective within these stages, and you are ready to draw up your first action-profile.

Remember that in the action-profile everyone has 100 per cent of

PGM behaviour for allocation. At this point, you can safely ignore the fact that some people are more active overall than others, because you are not attempting comparisons between profiles. You are not trying to assess some level of good or bad in the PGM pattern, or rate it by some standard of desirability or undesirability. You have to forget moral judgments, when drawing your profiles, because nothing is good or bad about a profile in absolute terms. It is not *better* to be mainly committed, or mainly attentive, or full of intention, nor is it *worse* to be almost totally wanting in one of the three action stages. In some circumstances this imbalance could bring excellent results!

You will notice at once that 'excellent results' does involve a judgment, and of course the results of actions arising from any particular pattern of motivation are open to evaluation. This is because the results of an action depend on the circumstances in which the action arises, and all of us have a share in, and consequently a responsibility for, the selection and creation of our circumstances and those of others. In the sentence above, it is only possible to say 'excellent results' because we also say 'in some circumstances'. For our present purpose, however, both results and circumstances are irrelevant. We are not concerned as yet to assess the results of action, but to understand its sources. How the action is applied in particular circumstances is not our present concern, and neither is judgment or assessment. What we are trying to understand is the individual's distinctive motivational pattern as revealed through his PGM.

Provided you steer clear of judgmental irrelevancies, the action-profiles are likely to give you a reasonably accurate reading of the motivational patterns of your subjects, even if you have not been in the habit of observing movement and your kinaesthetic sense is rusty with disuse. Most people find their own profiles the most difficult to construct, but are often accurate about their family, subordinates, employer, or friends. Once in a while, you may come across someone whose PGM pattern is obscure – in which case you had better abandon the attempt to draw that particular profile. Otherwise you should draw a profile as carefully as you can, and then test your results against the other information you have about the person you are profiling. Does your profile fit in with what you know or can find out about his work experience, life-style, accomplishments, and choice of hobbies, spouse and friends? If it checks out, then you have crystallized your understanding of behaviour in a way that can be valuable in all walks of life.

Drawing your first action-profile

Let us suppose that you have studied your Aunt Bertha's movement with care, and have made your notes on her PGM pattern. You must now draw up your first action-profile.

1   Start by listing the three stages of action, and fill in beside each a percentage allocation of the action energy which you feel is appropriate from what you have observed. For example:

Attention   45%
Intention   27%
Commitment   28%

2   Now divide each of these action stages into the assertion–perspective states in which they are expressed and subdivide your percentage allocations:

Attention (45%) { Investigation 20%

Exploration 25%

Intention (27%) { Determination 2%

Confrontation 25%

Commitment (28%) { Decision 20%

Anticipation 8%

This is your first profile. We do not know your Aunt Bertha, so the allocations we have used have come from a perfectly genuine profile, chosen from the many we have carried out. This means that you can check your reading of this profile against the information we can give you about its owner.

3 Now read your profile. What do you think are its most important features, and what conclusions can you draw?

You will notice at once that this person's profile reveals a high degree of motivation towards attention of the exploratory type, and towards intention of the confronting nature. It also shows a markedly low score for determination, and anticipation. Seeing this, you will probably be able to draw the correct conclusions. Here you have someone who has proved very good at making changes and is highly motivated to accept alternatives, but whose life-style has also been to follow the line of least resistance due to his almost complete lack of determination. As a corollary of his ability to change and confront new circumstances, he has been prevented from persisting in any one field of endeavour. His decision motivation has been strong enough to make him a good opportunist, but he has not felt that he must have a long-term objective, or project the outcome of present activities far into the future, as you would expect from his low anticipatory score.

It took a long time to discover the difference between male and female! Obvious though it may seem to those educated in the facts of life, the distinction in body movement terms belongs entirely to the way movement 'flows'. The assertion states (investigation, determination, decision) flow either more or less freely, while the perspective states (exploration, confrontation, anticipation) flow in terms of getting bigger or smaller. It is in the way the two relate together which express masculinity or femininity in terms of movement. You probably do not need to know this to make your own judgments. At least we have learnt that there is no exclusive type of action-profile which belongs solely to men!

Attention (52%)
- Investigation 40%
- Exploration 12%

Intention (25%)
- Determination 22%
- Confrontation 3%

Commitment (23%) $\begin{cases} \text{Decision } 18\% \\[1em] \text{Anticipation } 5\% \end{cases}$

Can you understand, as you read this profile, what motivation is strongest in this person? You can probably see right away that he is primarily motivated to assert attention, and is also relatively strong on determining and deciding. You will not be surprised to hear that he is an accountant with a reputation for vigilance. You will judge correctly that he loves his job, and suspect that his colleagues find him assertive.

As it happens, this was exactly the way in which his colleagues did describe him when they were interviewed. You can see that he scores very low indeed in all the perspective area, so it will come as no surprise to you to be told that he is inclined to barge into meetings that are none of his business. Since he is very low on anticipation, you will guess that he is a penetrating and meticulous fact-finder, but cannot be trusted as a far-sighted financial planner.

Both the people we have looked at have been strongly motivated to different types of attention. Contrast the profile below with theirs, and you will see that it belongs to a man who is quite differently motivated – towards determining and anticipating. He scores low in the attention area.

Attention (15%)	{ Investigation 5%
	{ Exploration 10%
Intention (32%)	{ Determination 30%
	{ Confrontation 2%
Commitment (53%)	{ Decision 23%
	{ Anticipation 30%

How, then, would you read this profile? Clearly it belongs to a man who likes to get to grips with something that can be pursued to a conclusion. He likes to project ahead the probable outcome of his actions and anticipate the results. His deciding strength predisposes him to set a fast pace, programme events crisply, and order priorities precisely. He gets a great deal done, but he is not selective or discriminating since he is limited in the attention area. He simply applies himself without question to the situation he happens to be in, and since he does not confront it, he is easily deceived as to the true nature of the circumstances.

Here are three genuine action-profiles from among the many we have compiled and analysed. Now it is your turn to draw up action-profiles for as many people as possible, cross-checking them with any other information you may have, so that you do not go off the rails while you are building up your experience and expertise. We have set out the full six-activity check-list below. You need to use this fully because it has been devised to be comprehensive, so that all observable behaviour is included in some combination of these six motivations:

1 *Investigating* defining; categorizing; fact-finding; defining standards and principles; establishing method, teasing out information within a defined area.

2 *Exploring* appreciating the scope of information; searching for

alternative possibilities; approaches and reasons; questioning assumptions.

3 *Determining* having firmness of purpose, determination and strong conviction; persisting against odds; resisting pressure.

4 *Confronting* crystallizing and establishing the importance of issues; challenging; recognizing immediate needs realistically; accepting hard facts in a forthright manner.

5 *Deciding* having a sense of timing; implementing action at the right moment; settling timing priorities, seizing opportunities; programming on the spot in a flexible manner.

6 *Anticipating* looking ahead; being farsighted; foreseeing consequences of action; evaluating practicalities, continually anticipating future developments; systematically planning for the future.

This list shows the strengths that lie in each area of motivation to activity. You can easily see by studying it, the advantages of each type of motivation. However, we must also consider the likely results of a low score in any area. For instance, if a person lacks motivation to investigate, the chances are that his actions will be taken blindly. You will remember that Aesop, who based most of his stories on the humorous observation of human motivation, and the quirks and oddities of its absence, told a story to illustrate just such blindness in action. In his story, Fox, always strong on investigation, went to visit King Lion in his cave, but on arrival refused to enter. Investigation of the footprints of other animals who had paid their respects to the invalid monarch convinced him that such visits were a one-way affair. This evidence was available to all the other animals except the first visitor, and yet they failed to investigate and went blindly to their deaths. Similarly a person who lacks exploring motivation in the attention area may plunge into disaster, because he denies himself the help, resources, facilities and new ideas that may be available. When Spanish courtiers complained that there was nothing much to Christopher Columbus's discovery of the New World, he agreed that exploration was indeed easy – as easy as standing an egg on end, which the courtiers found impossible until Columbus tapped the end lightly and balanced it on the indentation. 'It *is* easy,' he said, 'when someone shows how to do it.'

These stories illustrate weaknesses in the attention area, but Aesop's man and boy, who rode a donkey to market, were full of exploratory attention. They explored all the possibilities of their situation, under the goad of public opinion, but proved lacking in determination to stick to one solution, riding the donkey by turns and ending up carrying it! The person low on determination is inclined to let things slide, taking the line of least resistance and allowing laxity and indulgence, just as the person low on confrontation does not define issues, and deludes himself as to the nature of the situation he is tackling. Damocles, who wanted to change places with Dionysius,

King of Syracuse, was apparently low on confrontation. Only the sword hanging above his head, brought him to realize the dangers of kingship and the price of kingly feasts and indulgences.

Again, Aesop's stories illustrate weakness in the commitment area. You remember that Hare entirely mistimed his start in the race with Tortoise? His lack of decision deprived him of achievement, but Goat's decisiveness was even more disastrous because he failed to anticipate the ongoing results of leaping into the well to save Fox from drowning. He should have foreseen that this irreversible commitment could only lead to disaster, given Fox's habitual disregard for anyone's welfare but his own! As Fox, nimbly clambering over his rescuer's horns to safety, pointed out, no one had asked Goat to jump in. In the commitment area, it was fortunate for Fox that Goat was strong on decision and low on anticipation, but fatal for Goat himself!

Circumstances and activity motivation

As soon as we have completed an action-profile, and understood the strengths and weaknesses inherent in a high or low score in any activity motivation, we can consider the effect that circumstances are likely to have on its owner. Environmental influences, which we ruled irrelevant to the compilation of the profile, become of prime importance when we start to consider how anyone with a particular motivational pattern is likely to react to a particular situation. It is here that we are able both to predict and to evaluate. We can say that in view of the motivational pattern revealed in a particular action-profile, its owner is likely to react in this or that manner, and we can also say that, given the particular profile, it would be better to select these circumstances in preference to those. The action-profile becomes a means of predicting probable future behaviour, and of making creative choices for the future.

You can see this clearly enough if you suppose that someone you know almost entirely lacks the motivation for a particular activity. Perhaps in the commitment area he scores under 5 per cent for decision, and perhaps also the circumstances put him 'on the spot' so that decision is required.

We now have a man without the motivation for decision but heavily pressurized towards this activity. You will appreciate from our examination of the nature of the PGM, that this is an insoluble problem. Studies show that in such circumstances the demands of the situation do *not* create the missing decision motivation. No decision motivation develops to meet the circumstances, or, to put it differently, your friend's PGM does not change. Only two possibilities remain. Either your friend is compelled to take decisions, in which case he will time them badly, deciding too early or too late, and coming increasingly under stress, or he will evade decision at all costs, with results that may be spectacular. There are many instances recorded in history where decisions have either been taken in a very bizarre manner, or, to the historian's ongoing bafflement, not taken at all. Historians rarely ask whether these extraordinary failures arose from the lack of a particular motivation in some general or admiral or politician!

It is, however, much easier to understand how a person may take some circumstances in his stride, but fail to measure up to others, if we recognize the immense motivational pull that conditions our behaviour. A person's motivation profile derives from his PGM pattern, and each person's pattern is an action expression of his individuality. The more we research the PGM pattern, and the action-profile that can be drawn from it, the more evident it becomes that, if the motivational pull contradicts the situation, something must give; either the needs of the situation are not met, or the individual suffers. In these circumstances, some will opt for pulling out or lying low, and some for sleeping pills and misery as they remain at their posts. Obviously, such contradictions are most likely to catch up with us in new or unexpected situations in which we have not had time to find an appropriate role, and on which we have had no modifying influence. The new situation is the one to which we cannot adapt, because it is the most likely to demand from us an activity to which we are not motivated.

Fortunately the reverse is also true. Since we are heavily motivated to sort out our circumstances to suit our particular activity patterns, a wise selection of these is likely to place us in positions where the demands of the situation do not find us wanting, but on the contrary strongly require activities to which we are as strongly motivated. This matching of circumstances to motivational pattern is almost certainly the basis for the most brilliant successes or achievements in history, and is acknowledged by such phrases as 'the man for the job', or 'the man of the hour', or even euphorically as 'L'Etat c'est moi'! For this matching of our circumstances to our action-motivations we are to some degree responsible, and the results of our actions can be evaluated, but the sources of our actions lie in our motivational patterns, and these are given. We are no more 'responsible' for them than for the colour of our eyes!

Action-profiling and interaction style

Until now, we have been content to show how an individual's action-profile may be drawn from PGM observations, and his motivation revealed. We have proceeded as though each person were the only boy or girl in the world, and lived in isolation. But it is only in print, and in theory, that we can ignore the fact that 'no man is an island unto himself'. We must now enlarge our action-profile to take account of the realities and make room for *interaction*. Earlier, we agreed that the interaction of people's postures and gestures created the effect of a dance routine, perhaps a *pas de deux*, perhaps a full *corps de ballet* sequence, and this interaction gives a new dimension to our action-profile, and new insights to our understanding of behaviour.

Activities in a social situation inevitably give rise to interaction, and the degree of this interaction is important for our studies of the PGM pattern. Put two people in a room together and the chances are that they will interact. If there is very little apparent interaction someone may complain afterwards, 'I might not have been there', but the heat of this statement belies it; there has been interaction in the deliberate refusal of recognition. Exceptionally, there may be genuine cases of non-interaction where the parties have been utterly preoccupied or disinterested, and there may be very little when the purpose of the interaction is narrowly circumscribed. For instance, no one would expect much interaction from the signatories to a will, where the legal preamble provides for the maximum identification of the parties and the minimum interaction:

Signed by the above-named testator as his last will in the presence of us both present at the same time who in his presence at his request and in the presence of each other have hereunto subscribed our names as witnesses.

We are left in no doubt as to who was in who's presence, but everyone could quite easily have been cold and remote. By way of contrast, consider this passage from *The Glass Bead Game* by Herman Hesse:

Designori paused briefly, and threw a glance at Knecht to see whether he was tiring him. His eyes met his friend's and found in them an expression of close attention and friendliness which comforted and reassured him. He saw that Knecht was totally absorbed; he was listening not as people listen to casual talk or even to an interesting story, but with fixed attention and devotion as if concentrating on a subject of meditation. At the same time Knecht's eyes expressed a pure warmhearted goodwill – so warm that it seemed to Plinic almost childlike. He was swept with a kind of amazement to see such an expression upon the face of the same man whose many-sided labour, whose wisdom and authority in the governance of his office he had admired all through the day. Relieved he continued. . . .

Here is a much more lively picture of interaction than is implied in the preamble to the will; it is vignette of intense interaction in behaviour. Clearly, there is a whole new dimension which is not yet comprehended in our action-profile scheme. We need to show not only how a person is motivated to act, but also how, and to what extent, he is motivated to interact with others.

Interaction may take place at any of the three stages of activity. If our activity is in the attention area, someone who is with us may or may not join us in our investigation or exploration. If he is similarly motivated in the attention area as we are ourselves, then he will probably feel that he is invited to share our activity. If, on our imaginary desert island, John's sounding of depths, measuring of heights and enquiries into flora and fauna had been observed by an attention-motivated native, no doubt with explorations and investigations of his own in hand, then he would probably recognize John's activity as valuable and one to which he could contribute. John would return to camp with a Man Friday in tow! But if the savage happened to have little attention-motivation, then John's activities would strike him as ones from which he was excluded, and therefore of a sinister, private and spying nature and he might return to *his* camp with John trussed for his cooking pot! Although the illustration is absurd, and we have not allowed for the cultural differences that might prevent the development of affinity or for the scarcity of savages with cooking pots, it does emphasize the possible extremes of interaction or non-interaction in the attention area. John, who is highly motivated to investigate and explore, may or may not be able to share his attention activities with someone else. If he can it is because two conditions have been met.

1 The other person has roughly equivalent attention motivation of his own.

2 He is, himself, motivated to share his investigating and exploring activities.

When sharing does occur in the attention area, then the style of interaction is one of *communication*. Its distinctive character is shared attentiveness. The people concerned seem to be closely in touch, and ready to interrupt or overlap each other in conversation, taking up each other's ideas, suggestions and information. It is as though a pool had been created into which the participants were diving.

This communicating style in the attention area is in marked contrast to the way in which people share their activity in the intention area. Affinity in this area leads to a style of interaction that we might describe as *presentation*, each person seeking out a platform from which to make a declaration, state a case, or put forward a point of view. If the aunt, on our desert island, should come across another aunt with

similar motivations to her own – perhaps the Chief Girl Guide herself – we would not expect to find them swimming together in a pool or sea of attentiveness, but mounting rocks to make statements to each other across a divide. In the intention area, there is no interrupting or overlapping, as each presents a case in turn across the no-man's land between them. If they go to sea at all, our intrepid aunts will launch separate rafts, and argue their course from their own mastheads, sailing under their own flags, but never taking the plunge together. Their sharing is in parallel lines, with no actual intermingling. Visiting from rock to rock or from raft to raft is forbidden. Every aunt her own platform, as it were!

The aunts will share their determining and confronting activities, as happily as John and the savage share investigating and exploring. The problems arise when the four of them meet up to review their situation. At such a meeting John and the savage are likely to feel frustrated, deprived, or annoyed by the behaviour of the aunts, who will make a determined presentation of their wishes and views, and confront them with this declaration. Their sense of being badly used, will however be matched by the aunts' exasperation. As the aunts see it, they have presented a sensible, definite and positive case for a certain line of action, without eliciting a proper response. 'Talk, talk, talk, that's all you get from John and that Man Friday of his', they will complain, 'Never get a straight answer. You can't tell where you've got them', and the like, while John and the savage will leave muttering 'Bossy things! Demands, orders, arguments. No idea of proper discussion. No sharing of ideas. You just can't get in touch with them!'

Teamwork, on the other hand, is the distinctive characteristic of interaction at the commitment stage of activity. This interaction style involves teamwork in implementing some opportunity towards a particular objective. It is a style of *operation*. If someone appears from behind a coconut palm on our increasingly well-populated desert island, and holds the tent pole while Jill hammers in the pegs, then, as they decide to erect shelter for the night, or anticipate a good night's sleep, they are sharing commitment activity. Someone heavily motivated in the commitment area is predominantly an operator, and galvanizes others to share in his doings. Together they take positive action to bring things about, implementing and organizing action on the spot. They decide and anticipate, and, as far as Jill and her helper are concerned, getting started is the only bit that matters, and communicating and presenting activities are a waste of time. People who want to interact with them in these areas make them impatient. 'Let's cut the cackle', they exclaim, 'Get going', they order; 'Clear the decks', 'Bombs away', 'Fire', and such phrases are the only words they have use for. As Jill hammers home the tent pegs, she cannot really be bothered with John and his savage who are going on about possible dampness, insect-infestation and probable water-sources, or to the aunts on the best methods of making desert island camps. She is having that tent up and a good night's sleep or else. Fortunately, the stranger from behind the coconut palm appears to be the same sort of person as herself, since she can only share her decisions and anticipation with someone who has equivalent commitment motivation. She can galvanize this stranger, but others who lack this motivation feel imposed on, label her ruthless or overbearing and stand well back, however much they too need shelter and a night's sleep! Interaction, in fact, is only possible for an individual in those areas of his action-pattern that are positively energized, and only in so far as those activities have sharing potential; it can only occur if another is similarly motivated to those activities.

We can now add interaction style to our action-profiles, creating a column of units alongside the activity motivations we already have. Figures 9.1, 9.2 and 9.3 are examples. The shaded area in the inter-action units shows the degree of interaction in a particular style. To emphasize interaction in these examples, activity motivations are no longer shown in full but indicated by numbers: 1 Investigating.

Figure 9.1 John: the communicative explorer and investigator.

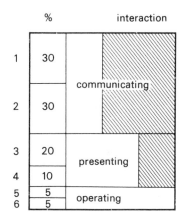

2 Exploring. 3 Determining. 4 Confronting. 5 Deciding. 6 Anticipating. The left-hand column shows the percentage allocation of motivation to these activities, and the right-hand column shows the proportion of interaction present.

You can see from Figure 9.1 that John's interaction with others is mainly communicative. He can also interact in the presenting style to some extent, but has nothing to say to operators. His interaction with others is quite, but not very, considerable.

Figure 9.2 Aunt: the presenter of intentions.

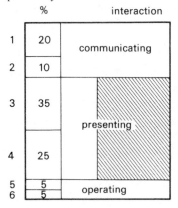

Figure 9.2 is the profile of someone whose interaction is in one style only; presentation. She cannot respond to a communicator or join in with an operator, and overall is not strongly motivated to interact with others, tending to be a 'loner'.

Figure 9.3 Jill: the committed operator.

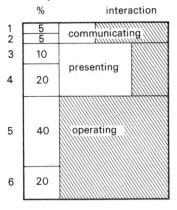

Jill's profile, Figure 9.3, shows that she is strongly motivated to interaction. Although she is mainly an operator, she is also fairly communicative, and also can respond to the presentation of a viewpoint, and is gregarious overall.

As you study this trio's profiles, concentrating on the degree and style of their interaction, you can begin to see how they will get on with each other, and with the other people on Imaginary Island. John is going to make a colleague of Man Friday, and will be fairly responsive to the aunt's plans, but he will not join in with Jill's operations in any way. She has almost certainly complained that she cannot see him for dust when there is something to be done! The aunt also leaves Jill severely alone when she is taking action, and gives an imitation of a brick wall if John is unwise enough to try and communicate the results of his investigations and explorations to her. However, she is not quite alone in her activities; the Chief Girl Guide is her partner, and they shine when it comes to a pow-wow on what should be done. At these conferences, she can put forward her opinions and respond to those of both John and Jill. The links between the trio, however, depend mainly on Jill. She must rely on the stranger from the coconut grove when it comes to taking action, but she can also respond to the aunt, and communicate with John. She will be impatient with them when she and the stranger are getting things done, but will not seem too overbearing because she shares to some extent in their activities. Fortunately John and the aunt are not alone on the island together. As a trio they stand a much better chance of survival!

Circumstances and interaction style

A desert island is a useful background for the study of interaction because it reminds us that sharing depends initially on individual capacity, rather than circumstance. Put Jill, who is strongly motivated to share her activities, on to a desert island by herself, and her temporary lack of companions will not affect her sharing-capacity. When she succeeds in hailing a passing boat, she will be the life and soul of shipboard parties in no time. Rescue the aunt from a desert island, and put her down in Piccadilly, on the other hand, and, with her slight sharing capacity, she will be alone in a crowd! A person's interaction motivation can range from 100 per cent (a fully shaded interaction column on the profile), to o per cent (a blank interaction column), through any degree in between, but you must remember that what is shown is not how much someone does interact, but how much he can. It is sharing-capacity that is shown on our profile. The greater the capacity for interaction, the more a person cannot help but see his activities as interdependent with those of other people; the less his capacity, the more he is a 'loner', whether he is actually alone or not, just like Kipling's *Cat That Walked By Himself*. This is true both of overall sharing-capacity, and also of sharing-capacity in relation to a particular sort of activity.

In any area of activity, there may be between o and 100 per cent capacity for interaction. If there is 100 per cent, then sharing may be experienced even in an action as limited as the signing of a will. If there is o per cent, then there will be no sharing, even if the object of a meeting were specifically designed to promote togetherness, as at a conference or in a group therapy. Someone like John who is strongly motivated to explore and to investigate, and also motivated to share this activity, will interact with other communicators like himself, but not with a group of operators or action men, since he lacks operating motivation. Among the communicators, he will experience a sense of identification, and among the operators a sense of alienation, which he will probably explain by saying that the first were 'a great crowd', and the second were 'not my sort at all'. On the one hand, you can have understanding, friendship, or even love, more or less at first sight; on the other, you have ice that will not break, and stiff, formal interchanges on the purely intellectual level, not to mention hostesses on the verge of nervous breakdown wailing, 'What went wrong? What did I do?' – to which the infuriating but accurate answer is both, 'Everything', and 'Nothing'. You probably will not dare to recommend the study of interaction to your hostess, but you can see for yourself how important it is for our own understanding of behaviour that interaction capacity should be recorded on our action-profiles.

Once you have included an assessment of interaction capacity or motivation on an action-profile, you can see how action and interaction motivation are related. If someone is motivated to a particular activity, then interaction in a particular style is possible, but this interaction will not occur unless there is also sharing capacity. If you feel impelled to do something, you may or may not also feel impelled to do it with others; the doing gives you the *opportunity* to share, but you also need the *capacity*. If John, who is 60 per cent motivated to attention-activity, had no capacity for communication, then in most of his activities he would be effectively alone. As it is, his profile shows considerable communication capacity, and this is the more usual situation, since people tend to be motivated to interact in those areas where they are most strongly motivated to act. Someone who expends most of his energy on investigating and exploring tends to be communicative, a determined, confronting person tends to present cases for action, and a decisive, anticipating person tends to take action, or operate. But we can all probably think of many exceptions, where a person's main activity is not matched by his capacity to share it. There are uncommunicative explorers and investigators, or ones like Sherlock Holmes whose mixture of secretiveness and oration tempt you to applaud his creator's murderous wish to topple him from precipices. There are some determined aunts who cannot put their viewpoints – tell that to Bertie Wooster – and there are action men who cannot accept partners in their operations. In such cases, action motivation is present, but interaction motivation is not, or is only present to a negligible degree. This discrepancy in a particular action area is shown on our action-profiles by a sizeable allocation of energy in the left-hand action column, but a lack of shading in the right-hand column. You can see this in the aunt's profile. She has no capacity for communication, even though 30 per cent of her energy is devoted to the corresponding attention-activity. Here the lack of interaction, or the failure to socialize a particular activity, arises from the motivational pattern of the individual, and can be read from the individual profile.

It is quite a different matter when lack of interaction arises, not from the lack of individual capacity, but from lack of the opportunity to *deploy* it. Like Don Quixote, you may have any amount of capacity for duelling, but you will have to tilt at windmills, unless you can find someone with a similar capacity to fight with. It takes two to fight a duel, and it takes two or more to bring about any particular style of interaction, all of whom must be similarly motivated to a particular activity and to the sharing of it. Accordingly, a person's opportunity to deploy his sharing-capacity depends on his circumstances. On the island, Jill's 100 per cent motivation to share commitment activities was frustrated by lack of similar motivation in John and the aunt. In the commitment area her profile shows a fully shaded interaction unit, while theirs is blank. She was only able to deploy her sharing-capacity as an operator when the similarly motivated stranger appeared from the coconut-grove; her sharing depended on circumstance.

We can say that a person's initial *opportunity* to share depends on his motivation to an activity; his *capacity* to share depends on his level of interaction motivation in the corresponding style; his opportunity to *deploy* that capacity depends on the motivations of others. In any particular society, a person may be denied the opportunity to socialize his activities, because of discrepancies between his own motivations and those of others. This discrepancy cannot be demonstrated from a single profile, but requires comparison between two or more action-profiles. Such comparison allows us to assess the opportunity for interaction available to an individual within his relationships, where the single profile can only show his sharing-capacity. In this way, we are able to take account of his circumstances.

We can now fit the three interaction styles into our action-profile scheme, defining them like this:

7 *Communicating* establishing and maintaining reciprocal communications; showing approachability; imparting and inviting knowledge and information; harmonizing and sympathizing; sharing processes of investigation and exploration.

8 *Presenting* maintaining confidence; making a positive demonstration; declaring intentions; influencing; persuading; emphasizing; insisting; resisting; sharing determining and confronting processes.

9 *Operating* on the spot organizing of people; creating a sense of urgency, or slowing down the pace; spurring people on, or delaying activity with awareness of objectives; controlling the action; sharing deciding and anticipatory processes.

And setting out the six action and three interaction motivations in a full action-profile framework as in Figure 9.4.

The nine motivations in Figure 9.4 interpret the PGM pattern – any PGM pattern. You can use this framework to fit in your observation of any one you like – yourself, your friend, your colleague, your Aunt Bertha or Uncle Joe, your employer, or employee. With it, you can translate his movement – his speaking silence – into words and describe his behaviour.

Figure 9.4

ACTION PROFILE SCHEME

Action motivations   *Action Sequence*   *Interaction motivations*

1 *Investigating* defining, categorizing, fact finding, establishing method, teasing out information within a defined area.

2 *Exploring* appreciating the scope of information, searching for alternative possibilities, approaches and reasons, questioning assumptions.

7 *Communicating* establishing and maintaining reciprocal communication; approachability; imparting and inviting knowledge and information; harmonizing, including sympathizing; sharing own process of investigating and exploring.

3 *Determining* having firmness of purpose, determination, strong conviction; persisting against difficult odds; resisting pressure.

4 *Confronting* crystallizing and establishing importance of issues; challenging; recognizing immediate needs realistically; forthright acceptance of hard facts.

8 *Presenting* maintaining confidence, making a positive demonstration, declaring intentions, influencing, persuading, emphasizing, insisting, resisting; sharing own process of determining and confronting.

5 *Deciding* having sense of timing; starting off a process of implementation at the appropriate moment – decisiveness in order of time priorities; seizing opportunities; flexible on the spot programming.

6 *Anticipating* looking ahead, being farsighted, foreseeing consequences of action; evaluating practicalities; continually anticipating future developments; systematically planning for the future.

9 *Operating* on the spot organizing of people; creating sense of urgency or slowing down the pace, spurring people on or delaying activity with awareness of objectives; controlling the action; sharing own process of deciding and anticipating.

The comparison of action-profiles

The comparison of action-profiles is a useful activity if you remember that profiles are not good or bad, better or worse in themselves, but only in relation to the circumstances in which action is taken. Useful comparison shows you how people can relate to each other and work together, and also how they should be teamed to achieve certain objectives. The circumstances or needs of the hour determine what sort of action or interaction motivations are valuable, and how they should be combined. If you set out on a project with some others, and you all have fully worked-out action-profiles, then you are in for an interesting time!

It might work this way. You are convinced that attention activity is strong in your profile, particularly in investigating motivation to which you allocate 30 per cent of your energy, and you are engaged on a work or leisure project with someone you think is low on attention activity, both in investigating and exploring, but strong in intention. As usual, you find yourself conducting enquiries and amassing infor- mation, while he is impatient to get on. Your motivation impels you to insist that you cannot move an inch without more information, and this impels him to insist that you know all that is necessary, and should move on more quickly. You are about to fall out, when you remember the action-profile. Hastily, you agree to get going while he agrees to continue the search for information. This, of course, is not going to work well, because both of you will find it difficult to resist the power of the PGM pattern. Fortunately, you realize that either of these solutions will make one of you ill at ease, no matter how hard you try, and sure to show it, even if you try not to. So you compromise. You collect more information – less than you think necessary, but more than he would like, and then you let him go ahead.

If you drop this colleague in favour of another predominant investi- gator, like yourself, you will find by the end of the day, that you have discovered exciting new ideas and bits of information, but are no nearer your goal. If there has been investigating interaction, you will have shared a most enjoyable communicative *rapport*, but you will not have determined on – or taken – any action.

While you and your fellow-investigator delay so happily, a friend decides to work on the same project with a colleague who has, like himself, a high operating motivation. They both enjoy getting things done, and whoever seems quicker on the uptake, more opportunist or closer to the ultimate goal elicits a response from the other. This pair of operators will undoubtedly get to the goal before you do, but only by taking risks, making some mistakes, and altering the value of the end achieved, by lack of discrimination in the methods of attaining it.

These experiences of working with different people will soon convince you of the way in which different individuals alter the nature of projects altogether, in order to bring them into line with their particular action motivations, and so you will be able to choose your team in a way that will be most likely to achieve the goal you have in mind, in the way you would prefer.

This is one very small example of the way in which you might put the action-profile to work. The action-profile framework provides you with a common behavioural language, which you can easily relate to your personal experience. You have to be careful not to misunderstand the definitions of the various sorts of activity, but this is unlikely to happen to you, if you base your construction of the profile closely on your observation of posture–gesture movement, and avoid treating it as purely intellectual exercise.

So far, we have only been interested in comparison between profiles in order to see how differences between them work out in practice. There is, however, one way in which action-profiles can be compared in the sense that they can be rated against a norm. There are three qualities which apply to the entire profile overall and which allow comparison on a rating scale. You can say that a profile has a greater, or less, *total potential activity measure* as shown by the degree of *dynamism*, *adaptability* and *identification* present. Different individuals have more or less of these qualities, and to obtain a full picture of behaviour these must be assessed, in each action-profile, on a scale. *Dynamism* is the measure of movement-intensity in a PGM pattern and is best thought of as a person's drive. *Adaptability* is the measure of a person's willingness to apply his PGM pattern in a new situation, where different customs, traditions and principles apply, and not to relapse into gestural or puppet-like behaviour. *Identification* is the measure of a person's willingness to participate in current activities – some people always want to be involved, although at any one moment it may not be practicable (you cannot dance with a broken leg, however much you want to join in) and others always remain aloof, even though they may want to be involved. Together these three qualities give the *total potential activity* of an action-profile, and this can be evaluated,

although the action-profile cannot be rated in any other sense. We must, then, add this to our total action-profile framework:

TOTAL POTENTIAL ACTIVITY MEASURE (*on a scale 1–10*)

10 *Dynamism* initiative in promoting action; drive in terms of exertion.

11 *Adaptability* embracing constant process of change; readiness to change own position, customs, attitudes to fit in with a new situation.

12 *Identifying* of self with the organization and its aims, traditions, methods, environment, personalities, with sense of participation.

and make the necessary ratings, if we wish to complete our framework for behaviour.

This chapter has been a workshop exercise, designed to give you a working appreciation of what you can understand from the PGM pattern, and to show in practical examples how the speaking silence can be put into words. Because our action-profile framework comprehends the entire PGM pattern, both our own, and that of others, everywhere that we have written 'PGM pattern', in this book, we could just as accurately have written 'action-profile' instead. The non-verbal PGM pattern translates directly into the explicit action-profile, and all of us have a profile, because we all use postures and gestures which merge to make up our PGM pattern.

The action-profile framework has been used by specialists for some fifteen years and the experience of using it has proved over and over again that it has real value. It works. It offers an elementary discipline for understanding the speaking silence of body movement, and it serves to establish a new theory of motivation that links previous ideas on the subject. Most importantly of all, it can help us to understand behaviour – both our own, and that of others – in a way that breaks new ground.

10

Silence speaks louder than words

This book has been in itself an activity that has followed through the stages shown in our action-profile framework. We set out to investigate and explore gestures and postures as the components of movement, examining the link between posturing and gesturing, and finding that each person has their own distinctive pattern of posture–gesture merging or PGM. These PGM patterns, we found, are expressed in our sophisticated, industrial society in a highly personalized form of ritual not characteristic of primitive societies, and reveal-

ing the motivational power of the PGM pattern. Our way was then clear to confront the problems of translating the PGM pattern into words, and we determined that this self-expression of the personality could be best understood as a pattern of action motivation. We were then able to implement action in our workshop chapter, and not only draw up the action-profile framework, but commit ourselves to working out examples and putting it to practical use. Throughout this activity we hope there has been interaction, which, as you already know, depends as much upon you as upon us. We have tried to make this book a shared activity, and we must now put it into proper perspective by anticipating its effects. What value, then, can we hope to derive from it?

We can now look at behaviour in general in a new light, and obtain new insights into particular behavioural patterns. For instance, as regards our own behaviour, our attempt to know ourselves is more rewarding than may at first appear. We now know that, since our PGM pattern is given more or less from birth, the person we are intended to express is ourself. To attempt to behave like anyone else, in the fundamental sense, is damaging, leading to behaviour that is

awkward and contrived, and putting us under stress. We are under a strong compulsion to be in harmony with ourselves, and this we should try to achieve. Our individual motivations to action are our unique birthright, and we do damage by fighting them, and act creatively when we try to understand and express them. 'Be yourself' is the burden of much philosophical and religious thought, and the lessons of the PGM pattern confirm it. We must learn to get in touch with ourselves, and avoid wishing to be what we are not.

This does not mean that we are not able to exercise choice. We are, in fact, strongly motivated to choose the circumstances in which we can express ourselves, and it is up to us to see that we do so in a way that ensures beneficial results. Our circumstances must be chosen to give the best possible expression to our personalities in creative ways and our choices are much more likely to be well aimed if we know who we are. In this sense we really do have a 'calling' to certain fields of action, and we have both our dharma or fate chosen for us from birth, and also the responsibility for choices that decide how this shall work out in our lives. It is as though we were given rules and equipment for orienteering, shown the first signpost, but left to work out our own routes. If we are aware of our own activity motivations and our interaction-capacity, we may have to do away with some fond illusions about the sort of people we are, but we will not waste time and energy on wrong choices in areas where we can reasonably hope to exercise discretion. The questions most of us have to answer include, 'What work should we do? Who should we love and marry? Who should be our colleagues and partners and what can they contribute? Should we work alone or in a team? What leisure pursuits are best for us, and with which friends shall we share them? What skills should we try to acquire and how can we best deploy them?' Our success in becoming fully ourselves depends very much on giving the right answers to these questions, some of which concern our skills and abilities, and some our relationships with other people. Our answers will determine our circumstances, and an understanding of our PGM patterns, as they are made explicit in our action-profiles, allows us to work out our answers with knowledge and good judgment.

So far, the benefits we are anticipating are ones that derive from your understanding of your own action-motivations, but many more arise from an increased awareness of such motivations in others. You can become far more appreciative of the wide differences between people and the ways in which they can, and cannot, be expected to contribute. Such understanding is mandatory for anyone who is responsible for the selection of candidates, especially if such selection depends on brief contact at interviews, and for all those who try to help others to choose skills, work, partners or other opportunities. Many people have professional responsibilities in these areas such as teachers, career guidance advisers, priests, personnel managers, industrial or commercial managers, social workers and many others, while some have such responsibilities in a voluntary capacity such as marriage guidance counsellors, and other good samaritans, and yet others have them as part of the general responsibility we have in society, as parents, relations, friends and colleagues. The more you base your judgments on a proper understanding of personal motivation, the less likely you are to found them on your own prejudices and self-interest. You will try to make an accurate assessment of the skills and aptitudes of the person you wish to advise or help, and you will know that people are by no means 'the same everywhere you go' as the saying has it, but on the contrary, are radically, fundamentally and involuntarily different from each other, with different needs and abilities arising from their unique motivational patterns.

Children, in particular, communicate their needs and abilities far more by their behaviour than by the spoken word. They 'say' who they are becoming, as they grow, and yet for lack of good 'listeners' their speaking silence goes unheard, and they end up by the hundreds as square pegs in round holes, making initial mistakes in important choices, because they have not had time to find themselves. It is far more important that they should be helped to understand who they are, than that we should keep asking them what they want to be. The answer to the first question makes it easy to answer the second.

In our culture, we give far too much importance to intelligence and to the spoken word. What really shapes our lives is not so much what happens on the intellectual and verbal level, but the underlying motivations by which skills, knowledge and intellectual ability are deployed in uniquely individual ways. The secret of motivation is in behaviour, and behaviour is expressed in movement, which has no tongue, but can tell us in silence how we can make the best use of our abilities, and relate to others. We have tried to learn this silent language, so that we can listen to the speaking silence in which this secret is told so clearly.

Silence speaks louder than words. We all acknowledge this from time to time when our emotions rise to a certain level of intensity.

'Words failed me', we say, when we describe the incoherence of anger, or shock or passion. It is when expression is most important to us that we find words most inadequate. You can say 'I love you', or 'I hate you', quite coolly at a low level of emotion, but if you are swept off your feet, or black with fury you will find it either impossible or unnecessary to say anything at all. Your message will come across loud and clear without words!

Words not only fail us, but they cheat us. We have already con-sidered the way in which even in a law court, where procedures are designed to obtain verbal accuracy, the participants still refer matters to a higher court. George Orwell in *Nineteen-Eighty Four* imagines the Thought Police checking up on people's characteristics, movements, and mannerisms to establish their sincerity. However, we must not push this check on sincerity too far! In one of his delightful 'Father Brown' stories, G. K. Chesterton describes the attempt of an ex-detective to check the importance of certain words to a suspect by his manner and how he obtained an incorrect result. Father Brown pointed out that the flaw in this experiment lay with the observer;

'You say you observed his manner; but how do you know you observed it right? You say the words have to come in a natural way; but how do you know that you did it naturally? How do you know, if you come to that, that he did not observe *your* manner? . . . If you could tell by his manner when the word that might hang him had come, why shouldn't he tell from your manner that the word that might hang him was coming? I should ask for more than words myself before I hanged anybody.'

This, of course, is quite right. Words cheat us, but we cannot check them by faulty and gimmicky observation of body language. We too need more than words.

The observation of behaviour, as we have shown in this book, depends on a rigorous discipline and a clear understanding of what can be properly understood from it. But it remains true that, if we are aware of non-verbal behaviour, we are much more sensitive, alert and informed about our situation than if we relied solely on words. A researcher (Albert Mehrabian) using a rigorous method of investigation found that at an informal meeting of the type that is designed to get people together to talk things over, only 7 per cent of the understanding reached derived from the actual words spoken. The new understandings transmitted at the meeting came 38 per cent from their intonation, and 55 per cent from the body movements accompanying them. On average, you can probably assume that about 40 per cent of the information you obtain about others is read from their body movements. This means that it is well worth while to improve your perception of other people's movement. Words in many situations are heavily discounted.

Words not only fail, or cheat, or prove unnecessary, they sometimes convey so little that it is better to look than to listen, and a great deal more interesting. Next time someone is being interviewed on television why not turn off the sound and see what impression you get, checking up afterwards with a friend who has seen and heard the interview? You may well find you have learnt more, by looking, than your friend has by listening. Although your command of language is the keystone of our civilization, and it would be absurd to suggest that we can do without words, which are after all necessary to the discussion in this book, we tend to get swept into a maelstrom of mass communication in which words are used meaninglessly or ambiguously, or are abused, or calculated to deceive. Writers like Hoggart or McLuhan, or Fowler have pointed to the degradation of language brought about by mass media, and the abuses of literacy, but few critics of words have suggested that you should use the language of body movement to correct, check and complement the language of words. This is what we suggest you should do. Next time someone says to you, 'That's what it's all about!' switch off your listening. This phrase almost certainly means that the speaker has nothing to say, and you will be better occupied in watching him, observing his body movements, and taking the first steps towards establishing his action profile. You will be better off, and a lot less irritated, if you spend the time finding out what sort of person he is, than if you patiently listen to dull predictable, and probably repetitive, buzzing. You may even find out why you are so bored, or he is so boring! If words seem significant and conversation sparkles, then concentrate on the words; if they do not, then it will be worth while to look – provided, that is, that you know how.

It would seem that the more we concentrate on words, the less we are able to look. An experiment was carried out with seventeen experienced interviewers, who were asked to interview a candidate for the first time themselves but, on the second occasion, to leave all talking to a colleague. As the particulars were already known to them, they were asked to switch off their listening and look. One failed entirely to do this, but the others reported that the second 'interview' had given them a quite new impression of the candidate. Simply by detaching themselves and looking, instead of listening, these inter-viewers gained new impressions that influenced their judgment. How much better interviewers they could have been if they had been able to base this judgment on an accurate evaluation of all the data relevant to the situation! They were not only deafened by words, but without a proper means of observing and evaluating behaviour. Such deafness often prompts men to express respect for 'woman's intuition' and to accept their judgments of people in preference to their own. However, there is no real mystery here. It is simply that the women have been more detached and so have perceived data also available to the men, but not perceived by them, due to their preoccupation with words. If the women become more involved, and the men more detached, it is the men who suddenly prove to have the intuition! The lesson is clear; if behaviour interests you, *detach and look*.

There are many dull or routine things we have to do that can be much more enjoyable if you are busy observing behaviour. Indeed it is often necessary to carry out your observation on just such dull occasions, because it is on trains, buses, planes or platforms that you

see strangers. If they cease to be strangers, and turn out to be people you know, you are immediately shackled by the tyranny of words, or swept away by a torrent of them, and cannot remain a detached observer. Naturally, you have to make an effort, because you would not normally be interested in passers-by, but you will find that what people do with their bodies is amazing, fascinating, surprising and interesting – but never boring. Forget how they are dressed, ignore the colour of their skin, their hair-style, height, width and all fixed attributes – you can even ignore their sex – but concentrate on the movement. Nobody stays still for long, although some will be restrained and some demonstrative; there is always movement which can be differentiated into posture–gestures and effort–shape. Fill out your observations of individuals by watching the pattern of inter-action between them, particularly in restaurants, or airport lounges, or other public places where you must often have nothing to do but

wait. By taking these opportunities which are available at the least interesting moments of your day, you will not only find new interest, but gradually improve your perception of body movements.

This leaves you with the problems of evaluation, but knowledge of your own pattern of movement will help you. How you see others depends on the sort of person you are yourself, and you must take your own action profile into account when you attempt to evaluate data on other people in an objective way. Even if you cannot avoid subjective likes and dislikes, you will know why people affect you in a particular way, and learn to understand them. This may not lead to liking, but will certainly lead to tolerance, and if you are in a position that requires you to make a responsible assessment of others you will be enabled to do so. You can succeed in making your enhanced perception of body movement a valuable asset as you look beyond words – into the speaking silence.

Looking beyond words means that we need no more words in this book! If we want to say: 'That's all for now; Over to you; Good Luck', without words, you will certainly know what we mean, won't you? You can hear the speaking silence, and read the body code and we know you will get the message!

Bibliography

This book has sought to show that to study body movement can be fun, beneficial and potentially significant. There are other books. The titles listed below indicate the broad range of disciplines and topics to which the perception and analysis of body movements can make a significant contribution.

ALLPORT, GORDON W. and VERNON, PHILIP E., *Studies in Expressive Movement*, New York: Macmillan, 1933.

ALTMAN, STUART A. (ed.), *Social Communication Among Primates*, Chicago University Press, 1967.

ANDREW, R. J., 'The Origin and Evolution of the Calls and Facial Expression of Primates', *Behaviour*, vol. 20, 1963.

ARDREY, ROBERT, *The Territorial Imperative*, New York: Atheneum Publishers, 1966.

AUBERT, CHARLES, *The Art of Pantomime*, trans. E. Sears, 1927; reprinted New York: Benjamin Blom, 1970.

BACON, ALBERT M., *A Manual of Gesture*, Chicago: Silver Burdett, 1893.

BAILEY, FLORA L., 'Navaho Motor Habits', reprinted from *American Anthropologist* vol. 44, 1942.

BARTENIEFF, IRMGARD and DAVIS MARTHA, *Effort Shape Analysis of Movement – The Unity of Expression and Function*, New York, 1965.

BARTENIEFF, IRMGARD, 'Movement and Perception', Plymouth, Macdonald & Evans, 1979.

BELL, Sir CHARLES, *The Anatomy and Philosophy of Expression as Connected with the Fine Arts*, 4th edn, London: John Murray, 1947.

BENTHALL, J., *The Body as a Medium of Expression*, London: Institute of Contemporary Arts, 1975.

BIRDWHISTELL, RAY L., *Kinesics and Context*, University of Pennsylvania Press, 1970.

BRAATOY, TRYGVE, 'Psychology vs. Anatomy in the Treatment of Arm Neuroses with Physiotherapy', reprinted from *Journal of Nervous and Mental Disease*, vol. 115, 1952.

CHAPMAN, A. H., *Put Offs and Come Ons*, New York: Putnam, 1968.

CHAPPLE, ELIOT, in collaboration with Conrad M. Arensberg, 'Measuring Human Relations: An Introduction to the Study of the Interaction of Individuals', Genetic Psychology Monographs 22, 1940.

CHRISTIANSEN, BJORN, *'Thus speaks the body'* – *Attempts towards a personology from the point of view of respiration and postures*, Oslo, Norway: Institute for Social Research, 1963.

CONDON, W. S. and OGSTON, W. D., 'Speech and Body Motion' in D. J. Horton and J. Jenkins, *The Perception of Language*, Columbus, Ohio: Charles E. Merrill, 1971, pp. 224–56.

CRANACH, MARIO VON, 'The Role of Orienting Behaviour in Human Interaction', in A. H. Esser (ed.), *Behaviour and Environment*, New York: Plenum, 1971, pp. 217–37.

CRANACH, MARIO VON, and VINE, IAN (eds.), *Expressive Movement and Non-Verbal Communication*, London: Academic Press, 1975.

CRATTY, BRYANT J., *Psychology and Physical Activity*, Englewood Cliffs: Prentice-Hall, 1968.

CRATTY, BRYANT J., *Perceptual and Motor Development in Infants and Children*, New York: Macmillan, 1970.

CRITCHLEY, MACDONALD, *The Language of Gesture*, London: Edward Arnold, 1939.

DARWIN, CHARLES, *The Expression of the Emotions in Man and Animals*, Chicago University Press, 1965.

DAVIS, FLORA, *Inside Intuition – What We Know About Non-Verbal Communication*, New York: McGraw-Hill, 1974.

DAVIS, MARTHA, *Understanding Body Movement, An Annotated Bibliography*, Arno Press, 1972.

DELL, CECILY, *A Primer for Movement Description Using Effort-Shape and Supplementary Concepts*, New York: Dance Notation Bureau, 1970.

DEUTSCH, FELIX, 'Analytic Posturology', *Psychoanalytic Quarterly*, vol. 21, 1952.

DITTMAN, ALLEN T., 'The Body Movement Speech Rhythm Relationship as a Cue to Speech Encoding' in A. W. Siegman and B. Pope (eds.), *Studies in Dyadic Communication*, New York: Pergamon Press, 1975.

DUFFY, ELIZABETH, *Activation and Behaviour*, London: John Wiley, 1962.

DUNBAR, FLANDERS, *Emotions and Bodily Changes A survey of Literature on Psychosomatic Interrelationships*, New York: Columbia University Press, 1954.

EFRON, DAVID, *Gesture and Environment*, New York: King's Crown Press, 1941.

EIBL-EIBESFELDT, IRENAUS, *Ethology – The Biology of Behaviour*, New York: Holt, Rinehart & Winston, 1970.

EISENBERG, PHILIP, 'Expressive Movements related to Feeling of Dominance' Rep. from *Archives of Psychology*, vol. 30, no. 211, New York, 1937.

EKMAN, PAUL (ed.), *Darwin and Facial Expression*, New York: Academic Press, 1975.

ELLIS, HAVELOCK, 'The Art of Dancing' in *The Dance of Life*, New York: Modern Library, 1929, pp. 34–63.

FELDENKRAIS, MOSHE, *Body and Mature Behaviour – A Study of Anxiety, Sex Gravitation and Learning*, London: Routledge & Kegan Paul, 1949.

FELDMAN, SANDOR S., *Mannerisms of Speech and Gestures in Everyday Life*, New York: International University Press, 1959.

FISHER, SEYMOUR and CLEVELAND, SIDNEY E., *Body Image and Personality*, New York: Dover Publications, 1968.

FRIJDA, NICO H., 'The Understanding of Facial Expression', *Acta Psychological*, vol. 9, 1953.

FROIS-WITTMAN, J., 'The Judgement of Facial Expression', rep. from *Journal of Experimental Psychology*, vol. 13, 1930.

FROMM, ERICH, *The Forgotten Language*, New York: Grove Press, 1959.

GATES, ALICE, *A New Look at Movement: A Dancer's View*, Minneapolis, Minn: Burgess Publishing Co., 1968.

GOFFMAN, IRVING, *Behaviour in Public Places: Notes on the Social Organisation of Gatherings*, New York: Free Press, 1963.

GOODENOUGH, FLORENCE L., 'Expression of the Emotion in a Blind Deaf Child', *Journal of Abnormal and Social Psychology*, vol. 27, Lancaster, 1932.

HALL, EDWARD T., *The Silent Language*, New York: Doubleday, 1959.

HALL, EDWARD T., *The Hidden Dimension*, New York: Doubleday, 1966.

HALSMAN, PHILIPPE, *The Jump Book*, New York: Simon & Schuster, 1959.

HAYES, FRANCIS, 'Gestures: A Working Bibliography', *Southern Folklore Quarterly*, vol. 21, 1957.

HEWES, GORDON W., 'World Distribution of Certain Postural Habits', *American Anthropologist*, vol. 57, 1955.

HINDE, R., ed., *Non-Verbal Communication*, London: Royal Society and Cambridge University Press, 1972.

HONKAVAARA, SYLVIA, 'The Psychology of Expression', *British Journal of Psychology Monograph Supplements*, no. 32, 1961.

HUBER, ERNEST, *Evolution of Facial Masculature and Facial Expression*, Baltimore: Johns Hopkins Press, 1931.

HUTCHINSON, ANN, *Labanotation or Kinetography Laban: The System of Analysing and Recording Movement*, London: Oxford University Press, 1970.

JENNESS, ARTHUR, 'The Recognition of Facial Expressions of Emotion', *Psychological Bulletin*, vol. 29, 1932.

JONES, HARRY, *Sign Language*, London: English Universities Press, 1968.

KENDON, ADAM, 'The Role of Visible Behaviour in the Organisation of Social Interaction', in M. von Cranach and I. Vine (eds), *Expressive Movement and Non-Verbal Communication*, London: Academic Press, 1975.

KESTENBERG, JUDITH S., 'Rhythm and Organisation in Obsessive Compulsive Development', *International Journal of Psycho-Analysis*, vol. 47, 1966.

KRETSCHMER, E., *Physique and Character An Investigation of the Nature of Constitution and of the Theory of Temperament*, trans. W. H. Sprott, New York: Harcourt, Brace, 1925.

KRIS, ERNEST, 'Laughter as an Expressive Process', Contributions to the Psycho-Analysis of Expressive Behaviour, *International Journal of Psycho-Analysis*, vol. 21, 1940.

KURATH, GERTRUDE PROKOSCH, 'Panoram of Dance Ethnology', *Current Anthropology*, vol. 1, May 1960.

LABAN, RUDOLF, *The Mastery of Movement*, ed. by L. Ullmann, 1950, 2nd eds rev., London: Macdonald & Evans, 1960.

LABAN, RUDOLF and LAWRENCE, F. C., 'Effort–Economy in Body Movement', London: Macdonald & Evans, 1974.

LABARRE, WESTON, 'The Cultural Basis of Emotions and Gestures', rep. from *Journal of Personality*, vol. 16, 1947.

LAMB, WARREN, *Posture and Gesture: An Introduction to the Study of Physical Behaviour*, London: Gerald Duckworth, 1965.

LAMB, WARREN and TURNER, DAVID, *Management Behaviour* New York: International Universities Press, 1969.

LANDIS, CARNEY, 'The Interpretation of Facial Expression in Emotion', *Journal of General Psychology*, vol. 2, 1929.

LANGE, RODERYK, *The Nature of Dance*, London: Macdonald & Evans, 1975.

MAHLER, MARGARET S., 'Tics and Impulsions in Children: A Study of Motility', *Psychoanalytic Quarterly*, vol. 5, 1944.

MANSFIELD, JOHN, *Selfscape*, London: Weidenfeld & Nicolson, 1975.

MASLOW, A. H., *Motivation and Personality*, New York: Harper, 1954.

MAWER, IRENE, *The Art of Mime: Its History and Technique in Education and the Theatre*, London: Methuen & Co., 1932.

MEAD, MARGARET, *Male and Female*, New York: William Morrow, 1975.

MEHRABIAN, ALBERT, 'Influence of Attitudes from the Posture, Orientation, and Distance of a Communicator', *Journal of Consulting and Clinical Psychology*, vol. 32.

METHENY, ELEANOR, *Movement and Meaning*, New York: McGraw-Hill, 1950.

MITTELMANN, BELA, 'Psychodynamics of Motility', *Psychoanalytic Study of the Child*, vol. 39, 1958.

MONTAGUE, ASHLEY, *Touching: The Human Significance of the Skin*, New York: Columbia University Press, 1971.

MORRIS, CHARLES, *Signs, Language and Behaviour*, New York: George Braziller, 1955.

MORRIS, DESMOND, *Manwatching*, London: Jonathan Cape, 1977.

MORTON, D. J. and FULLER, D. D., *Human Locomotion and Body Form*, Baltimore: Williams & Watkins, 1952.

MOSHER, JOSEPH A., *The Essentials of Effective Gesture*, New York: Macmillan, 1916.

NORTH, MARION, *Movement Education*, London: Macdonald & Evans, 1973.

OXEDINE, JOSEPH B., *Psychology of Motor Learning*, New York: Appleton-Century-Crofts, 1968.

PARNELL, R. W., *Behaviour and Physique*, London: Edward Arnold, 1956.

PRESTON, VALERIE, *A Handbook for Modern Educational Dance*, London: Macdonald & Evans, 1963.

RAMSDEN, PAMELA J., *Top Team Planning: The Power of Individual Motivation in Management*, London: Associated Business Programmes, 1973.

ROSE, CAROL-LYNNE, *Action Profiling: Movement Awareness for Better Management*, Plymouth: Macdonald & Evans, 1978.

ROWAN, BETTY, *Learning through Movement*, New York: Teachers College Press, Columbia University, 1963.

RUESCH, JURGEN, *Disturbed Communication: The Clinical Assessment of Normal and Pathological Communicative Behaviour*, New York: Norton, 1957.

SCHEFLEN, ALBERT E., *Body Language and Social Order*, New York: Prentice-Hall, 1972.

SCHEFLEN, ALBERT E., *Communicative Behaviour and Meaning*, New York: Doubleday, 1975.

SCHLIDER, PAUL, *The Image and Appearance of the Human Body*, London: Routledge & Kegan Paul, 1935.

SCHLOSBERG, HAROLD, 'Three Dimensions of Emotion', *Psychological Review*, vol. 61, March 1964.

SHAWN, TED, *Every Little Movement: A Book about Francois Delsarte*, M. Witmark & Sons, 1910. Reprinted New York: Dance Horizons, 1963.

SHELDON, W. H., in collaboration with S. S. Stevens, *The Varieties of Temperament: A Psychology of Constitutional Differences*, New York: Harper, 1942.

SKINNER, B. F., *Science and Human Behaviour*, London: Macmillan, 1953.

SOMMER, ROBERT, *Personal Space: The Behavioural Basis of Design*, Englewood Cliffs: Prentice-Hall, 1969.

SPITZ, RENE A., with the assistance of K. M. Wolf, 'The Smiling Response', A contribution to the Ontogenesis of Social Relations. *Genetic Psychology Monographs*, vol. 34, 1946.

TAGIURI, RENATO, and PETRULLO, LUIGI (eds.) *Personal and Interpersonal Behaviour*, Stanford, California: Stanford University Press, 1958.

TAKALA, MARTTI, 'Studies of Psychomotor Personality Tests, I', *Annales Academie Scientiarum Fennicae* Sarja-Ser. B Nide Tom 81, 2; 1953.

TEGG, WILLIAM, *Meetings and Greetings: The Salutations, Obeisances and Courtesies of Nations*, London: William Tegg, 1877.

TRICKER, R. A. R. and TRICKER, B. J. K., *The Science of Movement*, New York: Elsevier, 1967.

WALKER, KATHERINE SORLEY, *Eyes on Mime: Language without Speech*, New York: John Day, 1969.

WASHBURN, RUTH WENDELL, A Study of the Smiling and Laughing of Infants in the First Year of Life, rep. from *Genetic Psychology Monographs*, vol. 16, nos 5 and 6, Worcester, Mass.

WOLFF, CHARLOTTE, *A Psychology of Gesture*, translated from the French by A. Tennant, London: Methuen, 1945.